The Rise of the American Corporate Security State

Six Reasons to Be Afraid

Beatrice Edwards

BK

Berrett–Koehler Publishers, I
San Francisco
a BK Currents book

D1275098

Berrett-Koehler Publishers, Inc.
235 Montgomery Street, Suite 650
San Francisco, CA 94104-2916
Tel: (415) 288-0260   Fax: (415) 362-2512   www.bkconnection.com

Ordering Information

Quantity sales. Special discounts are available on quantity purchases by corporations, associations, and others. For details, contact the "Special Sales Department" at the Berrett-Koehler address above.

Individual sales. Berrett-Koehler publications are available through most bookstores. They can also be ordered directly from Berrett-Koehler: Tel: (800) 929-2929; Fax: (802) 864-7626; www.bkconnection.com

Orders for college textbook/course adoption use. Please contact Berrett-Koehler: Tel: (800) 929-2929; Fax: (802) 864-7626.

Orders by U.S. trade bookstores and wholesalers. Please contact Ingram Publisher Services, Tel: (800) 509-4887; Fax: (800) 838-1149; E-mail: customer.service@ingram publisherservices.com; or visit www.ingrampublisherservices.com/Ordering for details about electronic ordering.

Berrett-Koehler and the BK logo are registered trademarks of Berrett-Koehler Publishers, Inc.

Printed in the United States of America

Berrett-Koehler books are printed on long-lasting acid-free paper. When it is available, we choose paper that has been manufactured by environmentally responsible processes. These may include using trees grown in sustainable forests, incorporating recycled paper, minimizing chlorine in bleaching, or recycling the energy produced at the paper mill.

Library of Congress Cataloging-in-Publication Data

Edwards, Beatrice.
  The rise of the American corporate security state : six reasons to be afraid /
  Beatrice Edwards ; foreword by Jesselyn Radack. -- First Edition.
    pages cm
  ISBN 978-1-62656-194-6 (paperback)
  1. Intelligence service--Contracting out--United States. 2. Corporations--United States.
  3. Business and politics--United States. 4. Electronic surveillance--Political aspects--
  United States. 5. Internal security--Political aspects--United States. 6. National security--
  Political aspects--United States. 7. Privacy, Right of--United States. 8. Government
  contractors--United States. 9. Security sector--United States--Evaluation. I. Title.
  JK468.I6E29 2014
  355'.033073--dc23
                                                                      2014002507

First Edition

19 18 17 16 15 14   10 9 8 7 6 5 4 3 2 1

Interior design and production by Dovetail Publishing Services.
Cover design by Brad Foltz.

For the staff and clients at the Government Accountability Project, who never met a windmill that wouldn't tilt.

Contents

REASON TO BE AFRAID #1

Average citizens are subject to ever-expanding surveillance
and data collection by the government-corporate complex.

REASON TO BE AFRAID #2

Control of information by the government-corporate complex
is expanding

REASON TO BE AFRAID #3

The separation of powers established by the Constitution is
eroding. Rights guaranteed by constitutional amendments are
becoming irrelevant. Reporting a crime may be a crime, and
informing the public of the truth is treason.

REASON TO BE AFRAID #4

The government-corporate surveillance complex is
consolidating. What has been a confidential but informal
collaboration now seeks to legalize its special status.

REASON TO BE AFRAID #5

Financial reforms enacted after the crisis are inoperable and
ineffective because of inadequate investigations and intensive
corporate lobbying.

REASON TO BE AFRAID #6

Systemic corruption and a fundamental conflict of interest are
driving us toward the precipice of new economic crises.

Foreword

By Jesselyn Radack

In the pages that follow, Bea Edwards shows the post-9/11 merger of corporate wealth and government power in the United States— beneath a thinning veneer of democracy. The book in your hands explains the way in which this private/public collaboration gives policy-making over to profit-seeking corporate interests, which then become a direct threat to our civil rights and our way of life.

Peace and financial stability are the first casualties. Increasingly, well-connected corporate directors, with their privileged access to military resources and the national treasury, placed the country on a permanent war footing even as they dismantled government regulation of their businesses. They made a series of decisions and actions that the public never considered, debated, or approved, even indirectly.

The Rise of the American Corporate Security State examines the way corporate power behaves when it takes a dominant role in government policy-making and explains the advent of endless war. For profit-seekers, war is desirable for three reasons:

1. It is extremely lucrative for some companies.

2. The withdrawal of civil liberties is simpler in wartime because people are frightened.

3. The public accepts greater official secrecy because the nation is under threat of attack.

War justifies the dragnet electronic surveillance of Americans; the government claims to protect us by searching for the terrorists among us. The government also justifies withholding information about its actions, citing national security.

To comingle private wealth and public authority, US elites are promoting an antidemocratic legal regime that allows the exchange of consumer information among the corporations that now own the nation's critical infrastructure—banks, power companies, transportation companies, and telecoms—and America's intelligence agencies. This new legal collaboration will provide certain private interests with the cover of legal immunity for their invasive surveillance. It will eradicate the remains of your privacy and deliver your personal data to the government. Should you protest or demand redress, you will find that you have lost your legal right to remedy.

As an attorney, I represent whistleblowers from the National Security Agency, who speak about the intrusiveness and illegality of bulk surveillance of Americans. And I, too, became a whistleblower at the Justice Department when I witnessed the slide of the US government away from the Bill of Rights into a morass of illegal detention and torture. In different ways, through different means, our government accused my clients and me of betraying the country. But the opposite was true. We remained loyal to the Constitution, while our government betrayed it. When we spoke up, the Justice Department turned on us. Every day, we experience firsthand the consequences of the government's unwanted attentions. We know what happens when your government suddenly notices you—and sees you as a threat.

Edward Snowden, of course, knows this, too. He is stateless because he exposed the extent to which our government has compromised our constitutional rights and promoted the joint operation of private and public sector surveillance—under the guise of counterterrorism. The significance of his disclosures cannot be overestimated. He is revealing the whole ugly antidemocratic project, and he came just in time. Bea Edwards's analysis explains why we must act on what he's showing us, and if we do, we can back away from the brink of permanent war and gross economic inequality where the Corporate Security State is leading us.

Preface

In the United States today, we have good reason to be afraid. Our democracy and our freedoms are impaired. Many Americans have lost their homes and jobs and will never get them back. Our pensions and our privacy are also gone. Most frightening of all, the Constitution that protected us for more than two hundred years from the tentacles of oppressive government and the stranglehold of private wealth is less respected every day.

After September 11, 2001, our government told us to fear foreign terrorists, so we did. To protect our national security, we submitted to unreasonable searches without protest; we surrendered our freedom of speech and association. At a staggering cost, we financed a permanent, mercenary military to patrol the world.

In September 2008, when the economy froze, the stock exchanges plunged and private firms began shedding jobs by the hundreds of thousands each week. The Treasury Department stepped in and transferred hundreds of billions of dollars in public assets to failing private financial institutions. The subsequent congressional inquiry determined that we were all responsible. We were guilty of irrational exuberance.

But now, taking stock years later, we have to recognize that no foreign terrorist shredded the Constitution. Nor did we, as citizens, bankrupt the nation. Powerful forces inside the country did. And worse than that: they intend to keep doing it. They have yet to be stopped. This is the real reason to be afraid: the rise of the Corporate Security State.

The Constitution gave us three branches of government to ensure that no one small faction could control the state. Each of them is failing us.

The agencies of the executive branch appear to be helpless before the rise of the Corporate Security State. According to the attorney general, the Justice Department cannot prosecute corporations that usurp our rights and rob us of economic security, and the Treasury Department is forced to protect these financial forces from the consequences of their own reckless "trades." The president, whoever he happens to be, releases triumphant photographs of himself saluting in a flight suit or watching a live feed of SEAL Team Six killing Osama Bin Laden. He gives speeches about America and its greatness and periodically runs for re-election in what is now a grotesque pageant of clowns.

The Congress is paralyzed by squabbles over the debt, much of it occasioned by endless, off-the-books warfare. In the fall of 2013, the whole thing shuts itself down, along with the rest of the government, for lack of funding, flounders toward the next political showdown, and finally produces a meaningless agreement with itself about the national budget. Increasingly, the American public despises the entire body, and one poll taken during the 2013 government shutdown showed that we preferred cockroaches, zombies, and dog doo to Congress.

The judiciary, which is the last to go, blesses the increasing intrusion of money in politics, and stands down before the revelations of a secret court operating behind a veil of national security.

The Corporate Security State is tipping the balance between the self-interest of a governing corporate elite and the rights of the rest of us to freedom, privacy, safety, and fairness. We can see the power shift manifest in six clear and evolving trends since 2001:

▶ **Average citizens are subject to ever-expanding surveillance by the government-corporate complex.**

Intelligence agencies, working with private corporations, gather extensive private data on *everyone*. Outsourced government has created a complex of private national security contractors who capture approximately 70 percent of the bloated national budget for intelligence and surveillance.

▶ **Control of information by the government-corporate complex is expanding.**

The Obama administration continues to overclassify information. In 2009 and 2010, the number of classification decisions exploded. Among the documents deemed secret is the one setting out the cost of our national surveillance system and its unconstitutional domestic intelligence gathering capabilities. We are obliged to pay for it, but we have no right to know how much it costs or what it does.

► **The separation of powers established by the Constitution is eroding. Rights guaranteed by constitutional amendments are becoming irrelevant. Reporting a crime may be a crime, and informing the public of the truth is treason.**

Since June 2013, we've discovered that the National Security Agency (NSA) has been routinely violating the First, Fourth, and Fifth Amendment rights of American citizens. The NSA has been doing this secretly for years, while the Justice Department uses the Espionage Act to prosecute national security whistleblowers as traitors when they try expose it.

► **The government-corporate surveillance complex is consolidating. What has been a confidential but informal collaboration now seeks to legalize its special status.**

Legislation permitting the fluid exchange of information about citizens between the national intelligence apparatus and private financial and infrastructural institutions is moving through the Congress.

► **Financial reforms enacted after the crisis are inoperable and ineffective because of inadequate investigations and intensive corporate lobbying.**

The major financial institutions, well-connected to the Congress, the Treasury Department, and the Justice Department, ensure that key regulations implementing reforms are either unfinished or ineffective.

► **Systemic corruption and a fundamental conflict of interest are driving us toward the precipice of new economic crises.**

After the financial cataclysm of September 2008, the Justice Department's refusal to prosecute senior officials of the corporations that failed due to systemic fraud eliminated any deterrent. The deceptive practices continue, and the next collapse is only a matter of time.

The consequences of these trends and conditions are moving us toward a world like the one portrayed in the dismal post-apocalyptic movies churned out by Hollywood. We are submerged in wars that never end, and the wealth produced by and in the United States skews upward in ever greater concentrations. We await the emergence of the world's first trillionaire and look forward to the fawning portrait of him in a glossy business magazine.

Such a country can only be maintained with greater repression of dissent and suppression of the truth. This is why the government is into deeper and broader surveillance. Instead of funding education and health care, clean air, and water, our taxes are paying for intrusive electronic monitoring—of us.

But the battle for equality and fairness is not yet over. Many of the laws that prohibit surveillance and unreasonable search and seizure are still in place. Although they are under attack, and they erode incrementally if we are not paying attention, we still have recourse to them. And they still protect us from domination by a faction—the danger most dreaded by the framers of the Constitution. We must aggressively defend them, and we must promote peace for the United States and the rest of the world. For the war we think we are fighting abroad is also being waged against us. If we deprive others of their rights in an effort to protect ourselves, step-by-step we forfeit our own rights, too. That's just how it works.

*No truly sophisticated proponent of repression would be
stupid enough to shatter the facade of democratic institutions.*

—Murray B. Levin
*Political Hysteria in America:
The Democratic Capacity for Repression*

PART I

The National Security State

The right of the people to be secure in their persons, houses, papers and effects, against unreasonable searches and seizures, shall not be violated, and no Warrants shall issue, but upon probable cause, supported by Oath or affirmation, and particularly describing the place to be searched, and the persons or things to be seized.

—Constitution of the United States
Amendment IV

CHAPTER 1

The Government-Corporate Complex: What It Knows about You

Reason to be afraid #1:

Average citizens are subject to ever-expanding surveillance and data collection by the government-corporate complex.

Halfway across the ornate sitting room, Julian Assange stands with his back to the door, drinking a bottle of beer. It is early on a summer evening, June 22, 2013, and the Embassy of Ecuador in London is hosting a small party to acknowledge the one-year anniversary of his arrival in need of asylum. While Assange stands chatting calmly about the future of his anti-secrecy enterprise, Wikileaks, few people in the room know that he is worried. Sarah Harrison, his principal researcher and confidant, is only hours away from slipping out of Hong Kong with Edward Snowden, who, at that moment, is fast becoming the most hunted man in the world.

Close friends and supporters of Assange mill around the room, helping themselves to the buffet and arguing about software and the state of the world—in that order. Assange himself, with his longish white hair and black jeans, looks slightly out of place in the scene, bordered as it is by stiff-legged, gilt-painted settees. After a year, however, he's completely at home here, laughing and joking with the security guys, lawyers, and hacker guests, talking thoughtfully about the escalating struggle for control of electronic information.

"There's a completely new creation in the world," he says. "And the battle is on for access to it."

He's talking about the electronic "pocket litter" that each of us collects as we cruise the Internet and use our cell phones each day. Behind us, we leave a digital trail that reveals our interests, our politics, our friends, their friends, our health worries, our finances and fears. As he speaks, Assange is thinking of Snowden and what he had recently revealed about the practices of the National Security Agency (NSA) in the United States.

In the course of his highly classified contract work for the NSA, the US intelligence agency, Snowden uncovered unconstitutional surveillance programs that trace and store the electronic pathways etched across the Internet by hundreds of millions of Americans. NSA surveillance also sweeps up and archives the metadata associated with phone calls. Snowden discovered that Americans are subject to dragnet electronic domestic surveillance and have been for years.

His disclosure of NSA domestic surveillance caused a Washington tailspin, and the search for the source was on. After he identified himself in a video filmed in a nondescript Hong Kong hotel room, US political pressure ramped up on the Chinese government. The White House, the NSA, and the FBI closed in, and as a Chinese diplomat later confided, "You don't know what pressure is until you have those sons-of-bitches breathing down your neck."

Even if everything else the Chinese government said about its role in the Snowden affair was calculated, that statement was unquestionably spontaneous and true. Snowden had the secrets to the Corporate Security State that was quietly metastasizing through US federal agencies and corporate management suites after 9/11, and he was telling them to the world. He had to be stopped.

In the world of national security and surveillance, the evening of June 5, 2013, two weeks earlier, was frankly horrible. At about 9:30 Eastern Daylight Time, a story by Glenn Greenwald appeared on the *Guardian* website, linked to an order from the Foreign Intelligence Surveillance Court (FISC) of the United States.[1] In black and white, the document showed that, at the request of the FBI, the FISC ordered Verizon Business Network Services to submit all telephony metadata in its systems to the NSA. Only the data for calls originating and terminating abroad were exempted from the order, which, until the *Guardian* posted it, was secret. The order would not declassify until April 2038, twenty-five years in the future.

Telephony metadata, an unknown phrase for many of us until that night, includes the phone number called, number calling, routing of call, phone number identifiers, time of call, and duration. Subsequently, we learned that the FBI gave similar orders to Sprint Nextel and AT&T. Through a secret and tortured interpretation of the Patriot Act, Section 215, the court allowed this data collection.

Moreover, Greenwald wrote the next day that the NSA used a program called PRISM to collect customers' data from Microsoft, Yahoo, Google, Facebook, and other online corporations.

Two months later, a new Greenwald article appeared, also on the *Guardian* website: "XKeyscore—NSA tool collects 'nearly everything a user does on the Internet.'" The article explained that the XKeyscore program sucks into its maw almost every electronic datum on the Internet about everyone in the United States. And more than that: analysts need no prior authorization to inspect the emails, Facebook pages and postings, tweets, and Internet browsing history of ordinary citizens suspected of nothing. Via XKeycore, analysts at the NSA:

> [L]isten to whatever emails they want, whatever telephone calls, browsing histories, Microsoft Word documents. And it's all done with no need to go to a court, with no need to even get supervisor approval on the part of the analyst."[2]

Imagine that.

Many Americans can't, really. "I'm not a terrorist," they shrug. "So why should I care?" Then they laugh at the absurdity of highly skilled intelligence agents reading their dopey emails. "Go ahead, but it's pretty boring" is the typical reaction.

I work for a small nonprofit organization law firm in Washington, DC, that defends whistleblowers: the Government Accountability Project (GAP). Ordinary people come to us after they report appalling things in the places where they work and are dismissed, disciplined, or demoted in retaliation. They're hoping we can tell the world what they told us (at the very least) and get them their jobs back (at best). Most of our clients are federal government employees. We work with food inspectors, for example, who report animal cruelty in processing plants and toxic chemical additives to your food. Our clients are UN police officers who witness and report rape and sexual abuse by peacekeeping forces. Office workers and agents at the FBI and the NSA come to us to document gross waste and abuse. As do traders and risk managers who see pervasive fraud at multinational banks and FDA officials who report drug trials faked by pharmaceutical companies. At truly repressive institutions such as the World Bank, our sources remain anonymous, but they also contact us by phone and email.

As a result, at GAP, our emails are not boring, and we do not want the NSA collecting them, much less reading them. Since the Snowden disclosures, we ask our clients to meet us outside the office, downstairs, and around the corner at Starbucks. We have to talk face to face as if we were subversives. To be safe, whistleblowers facing retaliation must provide their evidence on paper now, not by email.

Journalists must do the same with their sources. Or they need complex, user-hostile encryption programs. The loss of freedom from unreasonable search and seizure that Snowden exposed means the loss of a free press and free speech, as well as a loss of freedom of association.

Those who shrug about all this are right in a sense. Most calls and Internet habits are attracting nothing more than routine attention. It is also true, however, that innocent behaviors can drop you into the NSA's net. You are suspect if you're communicating over email in a language other than the one of the region you're in or if you're using encryption (in other words, trying to protect your privacy). Dissenting actions will also attract attention: writing a critical blog, or book; becoming a vocal whistleblower, whether wittingly or otherwise; contacting someone who contacts someone else who appears to be suspect. And then you must consider that US intelligence agencies have on record virtually everything you have done for five years past.

You should know that whatever information about you the government lacks, private corporations probably can provide. Your bank, of course, controls your financial data: number of bank accounts, balance, history of deposits, how much and when, cash withdrawals, bills paid, and checks written. Everything you bought with your debit card is also on record. Of course, if your bank issued your credit cards, then your purchases and payments every day, every month, are collected there, too.

You may also have noticed that whenever you shop online for, say, a how-to book or a garden tool, however specialized, you begin to get emails advertizing different versions of these things. Pop-up ads seem especially tailored for you. That's because they are. Commercial websites use cookies that record the ads you click on so that targeting is extremely precise.[3]

Then there's the new industry of data aggregation led by corporations like Acxiom and ChoicePoint. In her book *Spying on Democracy*, Heidi Boghosian describes this growing enterprise, which collects information about you available from municipal service providers, voter registration lists, property files, and court records. Clients of these companies include financial institutions, telecommunications companies, and insurance companies, which buy profiles and records for direct marketing purposes.

The US government also contracts data aggregators. According to Bogoshian:

> Consumers are largely in the dark about the extent to which their personal data is being shared among different industries and government agencies and for what purpose. What is known, however, is that businesses and other organizations expend more than $2 billion annually to purchase personal information on individuals.[4]

This is what Julian Assange meant when he said that there is a new creation in the world, and the struggle is on for access to it and control of it.

On a Wednesday afternoon in the fall of 2011, Jesselyn Radack (GAP's National Security and Human Rights program director), Kathleen McClellan (GAP's National Security counsel), and attorneys from three nongovernmental organizations (NGOs) convene in the conference room at GAP. It is decorated with the customary law firm props: the long oval table, the speaker phone, and shelves of matching leather-bound law books that no one has opened since the advent of electronic communication. GAP's national security program clients (Tom Drake, Bill Binney, and Kirk Wiebe) are there, too. Like Snowden, they're NSA whistleblowers, but they preceded him and used internal reporting channels, all of which failed them and left them exposed to devastating reprisal.

This afternoon, at Radack's and McClellan's behest, they are explaining what has been happening to all Americans since 9/11. The lawyers sit along one side of the table, and the NSA guys sit along the other. Radack opens the meeting: GAP is making the NSA whistleblowers available to the group because their knowledge about the US government's invasion of Americans' privacy is fundamental to any meaningful overall defense of the civil rights of US citizens. Bill is the mathematician of the trio, she

7

explains. Tom knows IT and NSA management, and Kirk translates the math into the programming.

As the NGOs take notes, Bill and Kirk explain how NSA eavesdropping has evolved and what the government can do now. The US government, they say quietly, can collect every website visit, every phone call, and every email of anyone in the country. All of this information can be recorded wholesale and stored in massive databases, to be queried if and when needed.

Binney, looking the part of a bemused mathematician over his glasses, explains in lay terms the capabilities of the NSA. He names an apparatus the NSA operates: the Narus Insight equipment. It can process 1.25 million 1,000-character emails a second. The NSA has ten of them.

All web information is collected, regardless of whether the transmitters are of US origin, and all information is stored for a period of years by the government.

NGO lawyer X protests softly. "But that's illegal," she says. "They've testified in Congress that they're not doing anything illegal."

"They're lying," Drake answers, looking at her as if she's new on the intelligence beat.

"To Congress?" asks the NGO lawyer Y.

Wiebe laughs softly and nods.

"Yes," says Drake. "To Congress."

"Jesus," from NGO lawyer Z.

NGO lawyer Y comes back: "But the FISA court would never approve that."

Wiebe looks down at his hands and says no more.

The audience for this presentation is not made up of novices. These are lawyers who are not naïve about official commitment to respect for the Bill of Rights. Still, they're stunned, and as the shock wears off, Binney delivers the *coup de grace*: although the programs are both illegal and intrusive, they are not especially useful for purposes of counterterrorism.[5]

It's clear to everyone in the room that Bill Binney knows what he's talking about. He and Wiebe, with their colleague, Ed Loomis, and others on the signals intelligence (SIGINT) team recognize a worthless program when they see it. In contrast, they designed a valuable one: Thin Thread. A miracle of signals intelligence, Thin Thread could scan through the metadata on calls and messages, identify suspect connections based on past intelligence and current contacts, and throw the rest of the data away.

Besides its economy, Thin Thread had one other compelling feature: it was legal. In developing the program, Binney and his team solved one of the NSA's most sensitive and difficult problems. They structured Thin Thread to separate US calls and emails from the rest of the digital heap and automatically encrypt the data to avoid warrantless spying on US citizens. If Thin Thread found that a US-based phone number or IP address contacted a known terrorist suspect, the agency could go to the FISC for a warrant.

When the NSA tested Thin Thread, the program immediately identified targets for investigation and encrypted the identities of US callers.

"And then you know what happened?" Drake asked during the meeting at GAP.

"What?"

"They shut it down."

There was silence in the room.

"But why?" asked NGO lawyer X.

The three NSA whistleblowers looked at one another. Finally, Drake cocked his head, and a pained expression crossed his face. "Too many careers and contracts were tied to a different program."

Given the fact that 9/11 happened less than one year after the NSA shut down Thin Thread, there was nothing more to say. For his part, Binney was extremely disturbed about the NSA's failure to deploy the program. Thin Thread was ready to go months before 9/11, and he planned to apply it in Afghanistan and Pakistan, where it would be most effective: he was (and is) convinced that if the NSA had put Thin Thread online when it was ready, 9/11 would not have happened.[6]

Documents Edward Snowden began to disclose in June 2013 tell the whole sorry saga of the NSA and its corporate partners in the years after 9/11. Both what they have and have not done.

Back on its heels and lacking a mission after the Cold War ended, the NSA got new life with the advent of the Global War on Terror. Its budget more than doubled. Billions of dollars now disappear annually into intelligence contracts. Before Snowden told us in the summer of 2013, we did not know how much the US government spent on intelligence. Now we know: $52.6 billion annually.[7] Of that amount, 70 percent goes to private corporations.[8] Because, as taxpayers, we who fund the whole business have no right to know what we're paying for, the setup is ripe for waste and fraud.

9

In America, there's a curious disconnect between taxpayer concerns about the cost of social programs and the cost of security operations and war. It's as if politicians don't notice that Medicaid and the NSA are run by the same outfit—the US government. If the government wastes money on health care programs for poor people, which, by the way, are publicly and constantly audited, imagine what's going on at the NSA, the CIA, and the rest of them, where much of the financing is secret.

The possibilities for waste in government agencies with few budget constraints and little oversight are almost unimaginable, and the one agency where the budget is most generous and the external oversight is weakest is the Pentagon. When he ran the Army's Intelligence and Security Command, for example, General Keith Alexander, who later came to run the NSA, presided over the Information Dominance Center, designed by a predecessor to resemble the bridge of the Starship Enterprise from *Star Trek*. It had everything: hardwood paneling, odd trapezoidal chrome and glass cabins, and a huge TV screen on the wall so the little man in the glittery uniform could monitor the world while sitting in his great huge leather captain's chair. Those who have been there swore that the politicians Alexander invited to tour the place could also sit in the big chair if they wanted.[9]

All of this, of course, was assembled with public money.

The US government, which is huge and cumbersome and bureaucratic, is given to cronyism and ineptitude unless subjected to meaningful oversight. If no one is paying attention, public money can buy props and toys to shore up the egos of generals. This has been repeatedly exposed, and yet there is no effective watchdog for the intelligence world or the Pentagon. Their money and their programs are classified.

This is why war is so profitable. When the country's at war, the budget floodgates open and secret money pours out, funding black programs that lack accountability. And when we're at war, anyone who brings up even the possibility of fraud in the intelligence world feels the full weight of the Justice Department come to bear against him—or her. We know this because it happened.

On July 26, 2007, in the early morning, Bill Binney was taking a shower when he thought he heard a commotion downstairs. He couldn't be sure over the rush of water. He pulled back the shower curtain and found himself looking into the barrel of a Glock. The agent behind it wore a Kevlar vest that read FBI, and the gun was pointed directly at his head.

"Whoa," Binney flinched and dropped back. He waited a beat. "Do you think I could get dressed here?" he asked.

Binney dressed quickly and hurried downstairs. His wife and his youngest son were home, and he knew they would be terrified. He was right. They huddled in the living room as the FBI raided their house. By the time Binney got to them, the ransacking was well underway.

FBI Special Agent Paul Michael Maric, whom Binney had met before, broke away from a huddle in the hallway and presented him with a search warrant: a thick blue document with a long list of articles the team could confiscate. On the list was the book *State of War* by James Risen, a book that documented secret domestic surveillance.

Inspecting the warrant that morning, Binney, a long-time veteran of the Cold War and the battle against totalitarianism, felt a chill. The fact that it listed Risen's book confirmed for him that he was caught up in a leak investigation that many at the agency were watching warily. Published two years before, the book contained information about surveillance that the author should not have known. Agent Maric allowed Binney a few moments to inspect the warrant, and then separated him from his wife and son.

"Out back," Maric told him and steered him through his kitchen to the back porch. There, Maric told Binney to sit and began interrogating him.

Maric's questions were specific, and he brought up details about classified operations, describing NSA sources and methods in the unprotected space of the back porch. Binney became increasingly concerned. Here was the FBI, pursuing information about security breaches and leaks, openly describing classified operations without precaution. Binney, a high-level NSA specialist, knew that if anyone's house was bugged by a US enemy, his was. The FBI, however, on that particular day, didn't seem to care.

The questioning continued, and the day grew hotter. Maric wanted a name. The agents were after someone, but Binney wasn't helping. He couldn't. He knew there was a leak investigation, but he wasn't Risen's source. Finally exasperated, Maric yelled at him: "Tell me something that will implicate somebody in a crime!"

At that, Bill Binney shut down. This was a home invasion pure and simple by armed FBI agents. He was being attacked by his own government.

The attack that day was part of a coordinated raid on the homes of three NSA specialists, and Diane Roark, a senior staff member of the House Permanent Select Committee on Intelligence (HIPSCI). It was an attack many years in the making. For much of that time, Bill Binney, who headed a cryptographer team, worked with his group to develop Thin Thread and solve the NSA's primary problem during the 1990s. The analysts had to makes sense of the ocean of data pouring into the NSA daily, isolate real threat information, and protect the privacy of Americans. At a cost of about $300 million for full deployment, Thin Thread came in under budget, on time, and up to spec. Bill Binney, Kirk Wiebe, and Ed Loomis were pleased and planned to deploy it.

There they hit a wall, and nothing moved, even as they went higher up the chain of command looking for a green light. They spoke with Bill Black, the deputy director at the NSA, and finally with NSA director Michael Hayden. Neither would commit to anything.

In fact, Hayden didn't want Thin Thread and would never use it, although neither he nor Black would say so. Even as Binney sketched out for Hayden what Thin Thread could do, the NSA director was asking Congress for an additional $3.8 billion to develop another surveillance program: Trailblazer. Binney and Wiebe got orders to merge Thin Thread's data sweep with the embryonic Trailblazer, now to be produced by SAIC, Bill Black's former employer. The initial amount to be spent on Trailblazer was about $1.2 billion, $900 million more than full deployment for Thin Thread, without the fine-tuning that made it legal or the real time analysis that made it effective.[10]

At this point, Binney, Wiebe, and Loomis began to suspect that a financial force was driving NSA decision-making on security surveillance. In April 2000, they contacted Roark at HPSCI and briefed her. Reaction from NSA director Michael Hayden was swift and furious. He transferred both Binney and Wiebe to the technology division at the agency, where they had less access to congressional staff members.

At the same time, Hayden sent a memo to the "NSA Workforce," informing the entire agency staff that if anyone else decided to report his decisions to Congress, they would regret it.[11]

Seventeen months later, on a bright blue September day up and down the US east coast, a cabal of fanatics attacked the World Trade Center in New York and the Pentagon outside Washington with a coordinated hijacking of commercial airliners loaded with passengers and fuel. The towers caught fire and fell. The Pentagon itself seemed mortally wounded, and the country froze. Like a scene from a sci-fi horror movie, lower Manhattan and downtown DC filled with panicked and fleeing office workers and then stood deserted. No one knew what came next. Across America, air traffic control grounded all planes, and the stock market crashed and closed as TV stations rebroadcast the second plane hitting the South Tower of the World Trade Center over and over again.

It's difficult to envision the complacency before and the panic just after September 11, 2001, in the management suites of the NSA. After the 1993 World Trade Center bombing, the jihadists had gone quiet here in the homeland, but that attack was enough of a scare to crank up the contract machine and bulk up the budget for electronic surveillance in an agency hurting from the end of the Cold War. By 2000, Hayden & Company weren't all that worried, they thought they could shut down Thin Thread and fool around for a few years with Trailblazer prototypes and PowerPoint presentations showing what SAIC was about to produce in exchange for $3.5 billion.

Then, with the shock of 9/11, the threat was suddenly real. Congress was asking questions, but Trailblazer wasn't ready and wasn't even scheduled to be for some years. So Hayden did the logical next best thing: he picked up elements of an espionage program that Binney had developed for surveillance of the Soviet Union and used them to spy on Americans. Because the 9/11 hijackers were based inside the United States, the NSA turned a program designed for foreign surveillance around and used it instead for dragnet domestic surveillance. The program soon had a new name: Stellar Wind.[12] And the alternative acronym for the NSA—Never Spy on Americans—was no more.

A precursor of the programs Edward Snowden revealed, Stellar Wind enabled wholesale surveillance of Americans beginning shortly after 9/11.[13] In effect, the NSA, with the blessing of the Bush White House and the Justice Department, secretly did away with the Fourth Amendment to the US Constitution just like that.[14]

The operation of the NSA after 9/11 is a cautionary tale about secrecy and profits. Senior managers made the wrong decisions consistently, and no one stopped them because no one who knew the whole picture, and objected, could talk about it. Those who did know and who tried to object were silenced.

As the 9/11 Commission reviewed the lapses in US defenses that allowed the attacks to occur, the phrase "connecting the dots" entered the popular lexicon, as in "The intelligence services failed to connect the dots." Nonetheless, in the aftermath of 9/11, neither the CIA nor the NSA seemed to concentrate on more effective dot-connecting, which was exactly what Thin Thread would have done. Instead, the NSA wanted Trailblazer, a program that merely collected billions more dots. After years of this, the operative question is: just how many dots does the government have about each of us?

The answer is: too many because Stellar Wind was the real deal. Trailblazer, in the end, became a string of big-bucks contracts for SAIC that never produced a working program. Stellar Wind, however, unencumbered by privacy concerns, was sinister in the extreme. The program ran for years, sweeping up hundreds of billions of data points on US citizens, as if we were all plotting subversion. The Bush administration, which authorized it, and the NSA, which directed it, labored diligently to ensure that the American public remained ignorant of what was happening.

Very few people in Washington knew anything about Stellar Wind. In fact, no one outside a small circle of White House, NSA, and Justice Department officials did. Nor did anyone outside the circle really know how the program operated, until December 16, 2005, when James Risen and Eric Lichtblau published an article in the *New York Times* exposing the NSA's warrantless surveillance. The article opened with a dramatic statement:

> *Months after the Sept. 11 attacks, President Bush secretly authorized the National Security Agency to eavesdrop on Americans and others inside the United States to search for evidence of terrorist activity without the court-approved warrants ordinarily required for domestic spying, according to government officials.*[15]

On January 29, 2006, there was a second news bombshell. Although it was an ordinary mid-winter day for most Americans, it was a disaster for the cadre of NSA insiders managing Stellar Wind and concealing the Trailblazer losses. The morning dawned cold and clear on the Chesapeake Bay as the Sunday edition of the *Baltimore Sun* hit front walks and stoops around the city with the most explosive story of the author's career.[16] Siobhan Gorman, then a reporter for the *Sun*, began publishing a series of articles that exposed the gross waste and incompetence attached to the nonfunctional Trailblazer surveillance program. Coming on the heels of the December 2005 *New York Times* article by Risen and Lichtblau, the Gorman exposé infuriated the upper echelons at the NSA.

At the Justice Department and throughout the intelligence community, the search was on for the whistleblower.

Ironically, the reaction of the Bush White House, the NSA, and the Justice Department to September 11 unfolded according to the classic terrorist strategy. Terrorist groups are relatively small scale when compared to their targets; their leaders realize that their isolated attacks—even one as spectacular as 9/11—cannot topple a targeted regime. The regime's own extravagant reaction to the attack, however, does the rest of the work. Struck by a bomb—or by an American Airlines plane—the liberal regime clamps down on dissent in ways that make it unpopular, until the formerly free citizens themselves protest. Then the regime spends its wealth on stiffening repression rather than on public goods, so that it becomes increasingly despised and hated. No longer does the government help finance jobs, education, and health care. Instead, it sends tens of thousands of previously harmless young humans to distant countries for obscure reasons, where they die ignominiously or return home useless and wrecked, needing a lifetime of care, which the government no longer provides, either.

This is, in all likelihood, exactly where we are.

CHAPTER
2

Official Secrets: Absolute Control

Reason to be afraid #2

Control of information by the government-corporate complex is expanding.

The top-secret world the government created in response to the terrorist attacks of Sept. 11, 2001, has become so large, so unwieldy and so secretive that no one knows how much money it costs, how many people it employs, how many programs exist within it, or exactly how many agencies do the same work.[17]

On July 19, 2010, the Washington Post published an investigative story by Dana Priest and William Arkin that revealed the expanding parameters of the security state. The information that the NSA and the Justice Department struggled for years to control was seeping out, despite the attacks on the NSA whistleblowers and the censorship and harassment of journalists.

The effort to conceal the government's secret surveillance programs undoubtedly ramped up after Alberto Gonzales had a brush with perjury three years before the Priest/Arkin story appeared. Bush's hapless attorney general nearly revealed in an open congressional hearing that there were more surveillance programs than the Senate knew about. Gonzales admitted to "other intelligence activities," beyond the so-called Terrorist Surveillance Program, in a testy back and forth with Senator Charles Schumer.[18]

The FBI raids on the homes of the three NSA whistleblowers and Diane Roark occurred two days after Gonzales referred to "other intelligence activities," and four months later, on November 28, 2007, the FBI raided Thomas Drake's house. Drake was the official who communicated with Siobhan Gorman at the *Baltimore Sun*.

The FBI incursion and search of the Drake house was the same drill as the attacks on the others: a dozen or so agents stormed across the lawn in the early morning. The raid lasted eight hours, and toward noon ABC News and Fox News drove slowly up the street outside and parked their large boom vans at the curb to film it. The episode was broadcast twice that night and the next morning. For weeks afterward, Drake had to explain to his friends and neighbors why the FBI treated him like a dangerous criminal, a spectacle they'd seen on television repeatedly the day it happened as well as the following day.

The FBI raids in 2007 were one of the first manifestations of the extreme steps the government would take to secure its secrets. After 9/11, the US Defense Department both expanded and tightened its security regime, but it took awhile to build it out and cover it up. According to investigative journalists Priest and Arkin, 1,271 government organizations and 1,931 private companies in about 10,000 locations across the United States worked on counterterrorism, homeland security, and intelligence.[19]

Despite the campaign promises in 2008, the Obama administration did not arrest the trend toward more security-related secrecy. In 2011, Obama's agencies made 92 million decisions to classify documents, a dramatic increase over years past.[20] The following year, the Public Interest Declassification (PID) board wrote the president about the dangers of increasing secrecy:

> At its most benign, secrecy impedes informed government decisions and an informed public; at worst, it enables corruption and malfeasance.[21]

The extent of information collected and stored at public expense—but withheld from the public—is astonishing. The PID board's 2012 report identified one government agency that was classifying one petabyte of new data every 18 months, the equivalent of 20 million filing cabinets filled with text, or 13.3 years of high-definition video.[22] Moreover, the cost of storing and safeguarding all of this is high: roughly $11.3 billion in 2011, up from about $4.7 billion in 2001.[23]

The knowledge we now have about the national security operations of the United States suggests that we've moved from an embryonic position—where data collection is voluminous and secret but disorganized—to a more sophisticated state, in which the government's information about Americans is categorized, searchable, and centralized. The national security picture exposed by Edward Snowden in 2013 reveals a domestic surveillance system that is greatly advanced over the one Priest and Arkin described only three years before.

The government of the United States has two ways to withhold information from us, and they overlap for good measure. The first is to classify government documents as confidential, secret, or top secret for purposes of protecting national security. Classification withholds information from disclosure if requested under the Freedom of Information Act (FOIA). A second method is to invoke any of the nine exemptions or three exclusions of FOIA, one of which withholds classified information.[24]

Shortly after he took office, Barack Obama committed his administration to openness and transparency. In choosing him to be president, Americans effectively showed their displeasure with the arrogance of the Bush/ Cheney administration, which concealed the machinations of governing behind a veil of secrecy and national security.

Obama was a Democrat, not a Republican. He was a progressive not a conservative, and he represented a younger generation than Bush and Cheney. He was to be different. He said as much in a statement released on his first day in office:

> My administration is committed to creating an unprecedented level of openness in government. We will work together to ensure the public trust and establish a system of transparency, public participation, and collaboration. Openness will strengthen our democracy and promote efficiency and effectiveness in government.[25]

It was not to be.

An assessment by the Associated Press (AP) in 2010 showed Obama using FOIA exemptions to withhold information more than Bush did during his last year in office, even though the Obama administration had received fewer requests for documents. The AP's review showed that after one year in office, the Obama administration had increased the use of virtually every FOIA exemption in order to withhold information.[26]

The record on the classification and declassification of documents is no better. Obama's own PID board wrote to him to say: "[P]resent practices for classification and declassification of national security information are outmoded, unsustainable, and keep too much information from the public."[27]

Thirty-three civil society organizations supported many of the board's recommendations and also wrote the president to emphasize the importance of the issue:[28]

> *[T]ransformation of the classification system has become a democratic and security imperative, and the critical moment in this effort has now come."*[29]

That was April 23, 2013. The moment came and went.

Despite these consistent signs of growing secrecy in executive agencies and the regular warnings from sources familiar with government secrecy, the Snowden disclosures during the summer of 2013 occasioned an uproar among experts on national security law, cyber- intelligence, and document classification. People did not know what to think when the enormity of the revelations hit them. There is no precedent for what Snowden showed.

The disclosures came one after the other in digestible increments: metadata, PRISM, XKeyscore, illustrated with slides and official documents. Nothing was simply the opinion of the whistleblower. All of it was documented.

Thanks to Snowden, everyone who read or saw the news anywhere knew, for example:

1. The US national intelligence program includes sixteen spy agencies that directly employ 107,035 people.

2. For fiscal 2013, the classified "black budget" requested of Congress by the White House was $52.6 billion. The amount far exceeded what we previously thought to be true.

3. The CIA and NSA increasingly engage in massive cyber-operations to hack into foreign computer networks of both allies and enemies to steal data and sabotage infrastructure.

Perhaps most unsettling, the United States has spent more than $500 billion on intelligence since 9/11, an amount that exceeds equivalent Cold War spending levels.[30]

In brief, the Snowden disclosures show that the Constitution and the government of the United States have parted ways. We are no longer a democratic nation of laws. That's new in America. We've had our differences about various presidents, and most of us have little respect for the Congress, but in general, the judicial system enjoys a certain deference, and the country—including our government—as a whole is the subject of devotion. We still place our hands over our hearts and pledge allegiance to the flag—and to the republic for which it stands. The perception that the machinery of the state—including the executive, legislative, and judicial branches—does not respond to the will of the people, actively conceals its law breaking, and when exposed, deceives in a coordinated and deliberative fashion, is a first in living memory.

The Watergate scandal of the 1970s was also a constitutional crisis, but it was confined to the executive branch. It was also confined to one president, Richard Nixon. When he was gone, it was over. The same is true of the Iran-Contra scandal. Ronald Reagan broke the law and defied congressional intent, but the legislature reacted when the news broke, and the secret program stopped.

This situation is far worse than that, taking in as it does Presidents Bush and Obama—two very different presidents—their respective Justice Departments and intelligence agencies, the Foreign Intelligence Surveillance Act Court and its judges, and the House and Senate Intelligence Committees. When looked at that way, it's difficult to name a strong actor with both the skills and the incentive to right the ship of state. No one in government is empowered to expose the totalitarian infrastructure at the heart of the democratic government of the USA.

The seepage of power from elected officials—such as the president—to the surveillance agencies appeared clearly in early September 2013, as Washington, DC, prepared for the October state visit of President Dilma Rousseff of Brazil. The White House planned a formal state dinner and a heavy schedule of meetings to showcase the close relationship between Brazil, the new powerhouse in the Americas, and the United States. The two governments also planned to consider an arrangement between Petrobras, Brazil's state-run oil company, and the US government to allow US companies access to oil deposits trapped under a salt layer in the Atlantic waters off the Brazilian coast.

On September 8, 2013, the Brazilian newspaper *O Globo* reported that the NSA had penetrated the internal computer network at Petrobras, according to documents released by Edward Snowden. The news provoked a furious reaction in Brazil, as negotiators realized that US officials had outflanked them by peering into the Petrobras negotiating strategy. It added insult to injury because documents released by Snowden the week before showed that the NSA had hacked Rousseff's personal email and that of her close aides. As the conflict broke into the open, the White House released a weak and meaningless statement that did not acknowledge the NSA's invasion of the sovereignty of a friendly nation and did not commit to holding anyone accountable.[31] Rousseff cancelled the state visit with an angry public protest, and in the United States, the press highlighted the fact that the Defense Department's statement in August, denying that the NSA engaged in industrial espionage, was a lie.[32]

The Snowden documents have badly eroded the legitimacy of the US government both domestically and internationally. No one in government, from the White House to the Congress, has been able to state anything close to a reasonable and truthful case for the clandestine actions of the NSA.

After the *Guardian* released the FISC order to Verizon Business Systems, President Obama told an interviewer that the court is transparent and that it is part of a system of checks and balances. The statement, aired on broadcast television, was preposterous. The court order is secret, and it is based on a secret interpretation of the law—an interpretation that one of the law's principal author's asserts is a gross violation of congressional intent. In this one exchange, Obama damaged the credibility all three branches of government. The executive branch, in the person of Obama, is either ignorant or lying. The judicial branch is secretly defying the legislature, and the legislature, which is responsible for oversight, is not paying attention.

Deputy Attorney General James Cole tried to help the NSA out of its credibility hole in the early summer. In testimony before the House Intelligence Committee, he described the elaborate monitoring and oversight that kept the NSA in check. He did admit, however, that: "Every now and then, there may be a mistake."

Not long after Cole made this statement, we learned from the *Washington Post*:

> *The National Security Agency has broken privacy rules or*
> *overstepped its legal authority thousands of times each year since*
> *Congress granted the agency broad new powers in 2008, according*
> *to an internal audit and other top-secret documents.*[33]

"Overstepped its legal authority" is WashPo-speak for "broke the law."

And, of course, James Clapper discredited himself as well as the NSA when Snowden's first disclosure exposed his lie of March 12, 2013, to an open hearing of the Senate Judiciary Committee. Senator Ron Wyden (D-OR) had asked him whether the NSA collects "any type of data at all on millions or hundreds of millions of Americans." Clapper answered unequivocally: "No, sir." Then he equivocated a bit and added: "Not wittingly." Two months later, explaining his testimony, Clapper made his now famous statement: "I responded in what I thought was the most truthful or least untruthful manner, by saying 'No.'" He then tried to explain his explanation by saying that he was confused about what Senator Wyden was asking. Subsequently, though, we discovered that Wyden's office sent Clapper the question twenty-four hours in advance and therefore gave him ample time to clarify it, as well as to compose his answer. So Clapper not only lied in answer to the senator's question in March, but he also lied in July when explaining his earlier lie.

By September, no one believed anything Clapper said anymore, but he nevertheless kept talking. One reporter opined that Clapper should be fired simply because every time he opened his mouth those to whom he spoke were left trying to parse what he meant by complex words like "yes" and "no."[34]

Perhaps the most disingenuous statements coming from government in the Snowden summer concern the value of a public debate about the desirability or limits of a surveillance state in America. First, President Obama told us all: "I welcome this debate. And I think it's healthy for our democracy. I think it's a sign of maturity because, probably five years ago, six years ago, we might not have been having this debate."[35]

Parsing that statement is useless, too. On its face it appears to be an allusion to Obama's predecessor, who presumably would not have been so accepting of the potential debate. Or maybe it expresses the president's attitude toward us: five years ago we were too immature to discuss our own safety constructively. In truth, however, Obama has not been open to a national discussion of US surveillance practices, either. Nor is his NSA director, Keith Alexander, who nonetheless told Senator Tom Udall with a straight face shortly after the first Snowden disclosures: "Now, what we need to do, I think, is to bring as many facts as we can out to the American people, so I agree with you, but I just want to make that clear."

For his part, Senator Udall did not respond graciously:

> *It's very, very difficult, I think, to have a transparent debate about secret programs approved by a secret court issuing secret court orders based on secret interpretations of the law.*[36]

The key word, obviously, is *secret*, and the context of Udall's observation is judicial.

The Snowden disclosures eat away at the legitimacy of government not only because they expose the extent of domestic NSA operations, but because they show the way the court system, in particular, is corrupted and used to provide democratic cover for the surveillance state.

The Electronic Information Privacy Center (EPIC), like GAP a smallish nongovernmental organization in Washington, DC, filed suit in February 2010 under the Freedom of Information Act against the NSA. After media coverage of a developing partnership between Google and the NSA in response to a hacker incident apparently originating in China, EPIC sought: "all records concerning an agreement or similar basis for collaboration, final or draft, between the NSA and Google regarding cyber-security."[37]

It would be an uphill battle. Section 6 of the National Security Agency Act provides that the NSA enjoys exemptions from the obligation to disclose any function of the organization or "any information with respect to the activities thereof."[38] The NSA issued what's called a Glomar response to the EPIC suit: the agency would neither confirm nor deny the existence of such records because to do so would compromise the security of the United States. EPIC appealed the decision in district court and lost. EPIC appealed that decision, too, and lost. The ruling of the US District Court of Appeals, issued May 12, 2012, is replete with legalisms and case law, but in the end, it is fairly simple. The NSA is exempt from disclosing to the American public any information about its organization, functions, or activities. The FOIA produced nothing from the agency—not even an email.[39]

According to the appeals court judgment, the NSA must ensure that Google's information systems are secure because US information systems depend on them. Therefore, nothing about the relationship between Google and the NSA could be revealed. One year later we all found that this argument was exactly backward. The NSA is not cooperating with Google to ensure that its systems are secure. The cooperation allows the NSA to install backdoors into the Google information system for purposes of dragnet surveillance, thus weakening the security of the entire program for everyone. The *New York Times* broke the story on September 5, 2013:

> The National Security Agency is winning its long-running secret war on encryption, using super-computers, technical trickery, court orders, and behind-the-scenes persuasion to undermine the major tools protecting the privacy of everyday communications in the Internet age.[40]

The EPIC court battle dragged on and the years passed, through motions for summary dismissal and appeals. Until Edward Snowden released NSA documents, we didn't know about this struggle. Unwittingly, many of us have already been defendants in a contest before the FISA court, when the NSA sought the metadata of the customers of Verizon Business Systems. And although we did not know it, we lost.

CHAPTER 3

The Constitution Impaired; the Bill of Rights Annulled

Reason to be afraid #3:

The separation of powers established
by the Constitution is eroding.
Rights guaranteed by constitutional
amendments are becoming irrelevant.
Reporting a crime may be a crime, and
informing the public of the truth is
treason.

Here in post-Snowden America, the language and the principles of the Fourth Amendment of the Constitution sound almost quaint:

The right of the people to be secure in their persons, houses, papers and effects, against unreasonable searches and seizures, shall not be violated, and no Warrants shall issue, but upon probable cause, supported by Oath or affirmation, and particularly describing the place to be searched, and the persons or things to be seized.[41]

The amendment, however, has an abiding intention and a context that are not-so-quaint. In the American colonies, it was an unpopular yet common practice of the British government to issue general search warrants for tax collection purposes. Law enforcement authorities and customs officials searched whole towns, house by house, in an effort to identify every taxable possession or activity. This practice was—and is—easily recognizable as the conduct of a tyrannical government, which gives law enforcement the sweeping authority to search anyone at any time for any reason. Or for no reason at all.

The new democratic government of the United States therefore explicitly prohibited this practice. And now, in June 2013, we find that the NSA is relying on general warrants from a secret court that take in the American population for purposes of bulk data collection. The lawyers can argue for as long as they care to about the legal meaning of the words *search* and *seizure*, but the intention of the Fourth Amendment is clear to anyone who speaks English. The government—law enforcement, IRS agents, intelligence agencies—cannot seize information about you or things that are yours without expressing first a suspicion of a crime and producing at least some evidence that you're the responsible party. The evidence must be presented to authorities in the judicial branch of government, who decide whether it is convincing enough to justify the issuing of a warrant. A warrant, under US law, must be based on the individualized suspicion of a crime. Dragnet data collection, like that conducted by the NSA, is equivalent to a house-to-house, door-to-door search, and as such, it is prohibited.

Despite this standard of American government, we have been told repeatedly since 9/11 that we must sacrifice privacy for security because we are engaged in the Global War on Terror. This is now a never-ending war. There is no final goal. There is no tangible victory, and after more than a decade of war, we remain right at the center of it—nowhere near either the beginning or the end.

America has been at war since 2001 in Afghanistan, where large numbers of US troops remain. The Afghanistan war is the longest in US history. At the same time, we fought an eight-year war of choice in Iraq, from 2003 through 2011. Polls show that the majority of Americans do not see either US intervention as victorious. This is because they weren't. Behind us, after years of incalculable loss, we leave corrupt governments of cronies nominally in charge of states that will not cohere.

We are war-weary, and we don't want another losing battle. Despite our politicians fear-mongering and saber-rattling when the Syrian government apparently used chemical weapons in the fall of 2013, 75 percent of Americans surveyed rejected the idea of a military strike on Damascus.[42]

The prospect of yet another Middle Eastern war does not appeal to Americans. On the contrary, we Americans tell anyone who asks that we think the economy is the most important issue, and we want to go back to work.[43] The general feeling seems to be that should peace come, for the first time since September 11, 2001, the attention of the US government could turn inward to infrastructure, education, health care that actually is affordable, work and environmental conservation. This is what Americans are hoping for.[44] They say so every chance they get.

In reality, though, it doesn't matter what Americans want. The wars are not ending. Only the ground war is winding down. The War on Terror is with us still, and it may well last forever. After all, we cannot ever defeat terror, and we cannot negotiate with it. Terror is a tactic, not a government or a group. No one speaks for terror. Expressing the conflict this way allows our government to slip a new enemy into the picture whenever it needs one. So, when talking about our new threat—cyber-terror—our enemy can be Russia, China, hacktivists, Al-Qaeda, or "those who would do us harm," whoever they are.

Even if we're tired of war, the War on Terror is ramping up. National security officers talk now of target lists and a new strategy for pursuing terrorists, known by the bureaucratic and denatured phrase "disposition matrix." The matrix is a database that includes the names of suspected terrorists, cross-tabulated by the tactics to be used against them. These may be indictments or secret operations, such as capture or killing. Those who have seen the matrix and helped compose it say it supersedes the president's kill list, setting out plans for the termination of suspects.

That timeline suggests that the United States has reached only the midpoint of what was once known as the global war on terrorism. Targeting lists that were regarded as finite emergency measures after the attacks of Sept. 11, 2001, are now fixtures of the national security apparatus.[45]

More to the point, clandestine electronic warfare is here to stay. This is the truly chilling prospect because this will become the war within. This war can be silent and invisible. We won't know where or when it is waged. We don't know who the victims or who the aggressors really are. We don't know the cost. We won't know the objectives because these are secret. More and more of our national wealth will be used to fight this war. This will be the war without end, the forever war.

There are good reasons to resist it because the past decade has shown us that even here, on the aggressive end, a war footing weakens our already tenuous civil rights. The president himself says, "I think it's important to recognize that you can't have 100 percent security and also then have 100 percent privacy and zero inconvenience."[46] He speaks as if we are about to be hassled by a flight delay or a traffic jam, but the difficulty is much more serious than that. Obama was speaking shortly after June 5, 2013, when Edward Snowden revealed the extent to which Americans are subjected to massive surveillance. The inconvenience to which the president referred is the massive, ongoing violation of the Fourth Amendment.

In practice, the withdrawal of rights in the United States—and perhaps anywhere—is not difficult to accomplish when people are frightened and they're not told what they're losing. It's especially simple to annul the civil rights of people who aren't using them and don't realize that they're gone until they need them. "There is no subjugation so perfect as that which keeps the appearance of freedom, for in that way one captures volition itself."[47]

In the United States, white middle-class people are not ordinarily mindful of their civil rights because, in the twenty-first century, we've long had them and are not often obliged to invoke them. We are not stopped and frisked. We are not detained for being in the wrong neighborhood after dark or in the proximity of a crime. We're not arbitrarily asked for our identity documents. We learned in school that our country was the greatest, free-est, richest, fairest nation in history, that our judiciary is independent, and that we have three branches of government checking and balancing one another—a structure that is extraordinarily stable and clever.

Most of us, though, learned these ideas before we were able to think critically. We learned them before we knew about the dramatic percentage of African American men imprisoned, before we saw unusual levels of economic inequality, shoddy health care for people who can't pay, and crazed homeless people sleeping in downtown doorways.

Most of us never had to put our liberty-and-justice-for-all convictions to the test. If, however, in these post-9/11 decades you should say or do something that drops you into the hands of the federal justice system, you will find that your rights to freedom of speech and freedom of association—as set out in the Bill of Rights—are no longer operative. Without these rights, you will be ruined before it's over, whether you are guilty of a crime or not.

I can explain.

In the winter of 2011, John Kiriakou, a former CIA agent, approached us at GAP for representation. He told us he would soon be indicted by the Justice Department for confirming to an investigator, who relayed to an attorney for a Guantanamo detainee, the name of a CIA interrogator who quite possibly extracted a confession from the detainee under torture. The defense attorney entered the CIA interrogator's name into his client's case file, and the Guantanamo tribunal put the document under seal. In other words, although Kiriakou did confirm the name, it was never publicly revealed. He believed, and we soon agreed with him, that although this information would imminently occasion his indictment, his legal problems actually stemmed from an interview he gave to Brian Ross of *ABC News* five years before. In that interview, Kiriakou became the first US official to reveal that US forces tortured their prisoners as a matter of policy. There was a torture program, a manual, a staff, training, and a budget. Kiriakou's real crime, then, was reporting a crime—torture—just as Edward Snowden's crime was reporting a crime—illegal surveillance. The Justice Department charged Kiriakou under the Espionage Act and the Intelligence Identities Protection Act for revealing classified information. The multiple charges could have resulted in his imprisonment for more than thirty years.

No one associated with the torture program—not those who designed it or approved it, not those who carried it out, not those who destroyed the video evidence of it despite an order not to—went to jail. Only John Kiriakou, who told the public about it, did. In the United States, reporting a crime has become a crime, and official secrecy can be used to conceal torture.

It is the Espionage Act of 1917 that the Obama administration reaches for when a national security whistleblower must be silenced. The Obama Justice Department prosecuted Bradley Manning, Tom Drake, John Kiriakou, and Edward Snowden, using this archaic statute, branding them all enemies of the state. Adopted during World War I to address the political hysteria directed at German Americans, an early version of the Espionage Act included a punitive program of press censorship, which, fortunately, died in the Senate during debate, even then. At the time, Senator Charles Thomas (D-CO) made prescient remarks about the measure:

> *It strikes directly at the freedom of the press, at the constitutional exemption from unreasonable search and seizure. . . . I very much fear that we may place upon the statute books something that may rise to plague us.*[48]

Truth is now treason in the United States.

At this point in our history, if a crime is an official secret, anyone who speaks about it is a criminal.

Our lack of rights is not apparent, though, because our form of government is unchanged. Civilians control the military, the president runs the executive branch, Congress approves the nation's budget and taxes the people, and the judicial system operates without visible influence from outside forces. The Constitution of the United States is intact, only impaired, but the Bill of Rights has been shredded.

In dissecting the loss of freedom, it is important to distinguish between the Constitution and the Bill of Rights—its first ten amendments. The Constitution *per se*, consists of seven articles that specify the rights of property, the responsibilities of the state, and the conduct of elections. Looking at the original, it is clear that the thinking behind it was ingenious for its time and established a government structure that would be difficult for any one faction to control completely, given at least some diversity of interests.

The actual Constitution—the original without its amendments—is ingenious because it ensures stability, but it's not all that democratic. Slavery was an accepted practice. Women could not vote. The Senate was elected by the state legislatures, and the president was elected by a college of electors. Only the House of Representatives was directly elected by male citizens. In most states, only white male property owners could vote. For well over two hundred years, in practice, only white male property owners held the office of president of the United States.

The rights of citizens came, first, through the Bill of Rights, which the Framers added as a concession to secure the support of yeoman farmers in the thirteen colonies who were not enthusiastic about granting a central/federal government the power to tax them. The Bill of Rights is what most of us think of when we express our reverence for the US Constitution: freedom of speech, the right to personal security, freedom of association and freedom from self-incrimination, guarantees of due process and habeas corpus.

Over the course of our history, we have democratized the state through constitutional amendments. Article XIII ended slavery, and Article XIV, passed in 1868, extended most of the provisions of the Bill of Rights to the states. Article XIX bestows upon women the right to vote.

Rights of people, then, as opposed to rights of property and privileges of the state, were added to the US Constitution, and therefore can be drained away without altering at all the form in which we're governed. We do not live in Lenin's Soviet Union, which had to depose the czar, or even in Pinochet's Chile, which assassinated the civilian president and installed a military head of state. The constitutional forms are still in place. Only our rights as individual citizens are weakened.

Joseph Nacchio was the CEO of Qwest Communications in February 2001, when the NSA approached him about cooperation with the agency's surveillance activities, seven months before the attacks of 9/11. Nacchio entertained the NSA's request for Qwest's customers' call records and asked the Qwest general counsel for advice. After reviewing the NSA request, the general counsel advised Nacchio that the NSA's proposal was illegal, and Qwest could not comply without a FISA warrant. Years later, of course, we found that the NSA had made similar requests of all the major telecoms—Verizon, AT&T, Sprint Nextel, and so forth—and Qwest was the only corporation to object. Nacchio claims that the NSA then retaliated by excluding Qwest from lucrative contract work.

Subsequently, the Department of Justice charged Joseph Nacchio with forty-two counts of insider trading. When he tried to defend himself against the charges by introducing the background conflict between himself as Qwest CEO and the NSA, the court ruled the information inadmissible.[49]

When ultimately released, court documents showed that during the crucial period, February 2001, Nacchio served as the chairman of the National Security Telecommunications Advisory Committee. The NSA approached him about a program called Groundbreaker, which would outsource much of the agency's nonclassified work. During a meeting, NSA officials also proposed another kind of cooperation, but redactions in the court documents obscure the exact nature of that proposal.[50]

Nacchio's defense attorney claimed that the NSA pressured him for months after the February 2001 meeting to grant the agency broad access to phone call information and Internet traffic on the Qwest network, but Qwest's attorneys warned him that if he complied with the NSA's request, the corporation could be guilty of a felony. So he responded to the agency that he could only submit customer data to the government if presented with a FISA warrant.

Subsequently, Qwest acquired telecom US West, and in 2005, the Justice Department charged Nacchio with accounting fraud for misrepresenting his corporation's bottom line in negotiations. In his defense, Nacchio wanted to claim that at the time of the purchase, he believed Qwest would soon prosper as the result of its participation in a series of lucrative government communications contracts. After he refused to cooperate with the NSA, however, the expected contracts did not materialize, and Qwest's financial position deteriorated.

During Nacchio's trial, none of this information was introduced because it was classified. Ultimately, he was convicted on nineteen of forty-two counts and served four and a half years of a six-year sentence.

Two things. First, whether Nacchio is guilty of a crime or not, his defense—once documents were unsealed—asserts that the pressure to provide the raw material for large-scale domestic spying involving telecoms began just after George W. Bush became president, well before September 11, 2001. If Nacchio were the only one who claimed this, it might be a fragile argument, but telecom customers of several corporations filed lawsuits accusing the providers of violating their subscribers' privacy beginning around February 2001. The suit filed against AT&T asserts that seven months before September 11, 2001, the company:

> *[B]egan development of a center for monitoring long distance calls and Internet transmissions and other digital information for the exclusive use of the NSA.*[51]

There is powerful evidence to substantiate the claim that September 11, 2001, was not, in fact, the incident that precipitated the broad sweep surveillance of Americans. Nacchio and the lawsuits against AT&T and other telecoms assert that the request for access to private data began virtually as soon as George W. Bush took office, months before 9/11.

Secondly, Nacchio's case shows what Kiriakou's does: the US intelligence apparatus retaliates through the Justice Department for noncompliance with its demands. As others have pointed out, if Nacchio's defense were untrue, why didn't the prosecutor allow it to be admitted and then expose it as bogus? Why did the defense have to be excluded?[52]

Five years later, we are no closer to knowing the truth. Part of the problem is that Congress is not pressing hard for answers. In the fall after the initial Snowden disclosures, at hearings called by the Senate Judiciary Committee, only a few senators, including Ron Wyden and Mark Udall, regularly asked specific confrontational questions of NSA Director Keith Alexander designed to elicit meaningful answers. Congressional oversight simply isn't there.

Although electronic surveillance of Americans receives much of the public's attention, other rights are quietly weakening, too. Most significant perhaps is the pending loss of the right to due process and habeas corpus. Under the National Defense Authorization Act (NDAA) for 2012, the president apparently acquired the power to order the military to detain

> [a] person who was a part of or substantially supported al-Qaeda, the Taliban, or associated forces that are engaged in hostilities against the United States or its coalition partners, including any person who has committed a belligerent act or has directly supported such hostilities in aid of such enemy forces.[53]

Anyone detained under the statute, may be held indefinitely without trial under the law of war "until the end of the hostilities authorized by the [Authorized Use of Military Force]."[54] Moreover, people detained would have no right to be notified of the specific charges against them and would thus be unable to defend themselves.

There is considerable controversy surrounding the interpretation and application of the law, and civil liberties organizations protest it strenuously. Chris Hedges, a journalist, and six political dissidents filed suit in federal court asserting a fear of prosecution under new military powers. Most realistically and immediately, they fear the law could be used to detain American citizens on American soil, accuse them of association with Al-Qaeda, and deport them for detention at Guantanamo Bay until the end of hostilities, whenever that is. The concern and confusion surround the phrases "substantially support" and "associated forces," and a number of journalists believe that the law could be used against them if they interview members of Al-Qaeda or publish information about them. If this could occur, or even be attempted, the NDAA (section 1021) violates the First Amendment (the right to free speech) and the Fifth Amendment (freedom from self-incrimination), at the very least.

In the most recent ruling on the lawsuit, the Second Circuit Court of Appeals upheld the implementation of NDAA:

> *Since the U.S. government has promised that citizens, journalists, and activists were not in danger of being detained as a result of NDAA, it was unnecessary to block the enforcement of 102 (b)(2) of the NDAA.*[55]

The judges apparently believe that if government lawyers assert something, then it's true. The ruling, issued on July 17, 2013, came one month after the first disclosure made by Edward Snowden that exposed the NSA's repeated assurances to Congress that the agency would not spy on Americans in an unwarranted wholesale fashion as a lie.

So here we are. The NDAA poses a real threat to journalists, whistleblowers, and whistleblower advocates, who may be detained without trial indefinitely for writing about someone who challenges government actions. The law is far from clear, and while the courts decide which interpretation of its nebulous phrases might be constitutional, its chilling effect is already obvious.

This is America in 2013, a country so far from its founding ideals that it's difficult to recognize. Those running the electronic espionage system designed to track foreign terror suspects ultimately turned their surveillance equipment on us.

Congress does not object. Even when lied to in open session while the television cameras roll, as Senator Wyden was, the Senate does not investigate. There is no special prosecutor and no effort to determine what lies beneath the lies. Why is that?

Because, in acquiring all electronic information there is to have about each of us, the NSA also acquires unlimited information about senators and congressmen. Who among them wants to find him- or herself in a pissing match with Keith Alexander or James Clapper? How can any one of them be sure there is no record of a dubious campaign contribution, a fund-raising call from a Senate office instead of campaign headquarters, a childhood friend who turned out badly, a quick trip to rehab, a struggle with online poker playing or pornography? As Willie Stark told Jake in *All the King's Men*: "There's always something." Any sensible politician would be afraid that the NSA knows what that something is.

This is the problem when the government—or part of it—knows more about us than we know about the government. In this context, information really is power. When a single secretive executive agency has it all, the responsiveness of democratic processes is compromised. Neither elected nor appointed officials can confront such an agency and survive the retaliation. Legislators in particular seem slavish when confronted with the potential crimes of the NSA. Moreover, the government seems to conduct itself in ways that do not accurately reflect the will of the electorate.

When we lose our right to freedom from unreasonable search and seizure, we lose the presumption of innocence. There's a reason we need that departure point in a conflict with the state and a reason we have those rights. They establish the sovereignty of the people as opposed to that of a dictator. They protect us from the tyranny of the state.

PART II

The Corporate Security Complex

Money talks.

—American Idiom

CHAPTER 4

The Zombie Bill: The Corporate Security Campaign That Will Not Die

Reason to be afraid #4:

The government-corporate surveillance complex is consolidating. What has been a confidential but informal collaboration now seeks to legalize its special status.

July 9, 2012, was a scorcher in Washington, DC, with afternoon temperatures over 100 degrees, when an audience of about fifty think-tankers convened in a third-floor briefing room of the Senate's Russell Office Building on Capitol Hill. Then-Senator John Kyl sponsored the show, although he did not appear in person. He had invited the American Center for Democracy (ACD) and the Economic Warfare Institute (EWI) to explore the topic of "Economic Warfare Subversions: Anticipating the Threat."

At the front of the room, under a swag of the heavy red draperies and the American flag, sat the panel. The lineup was peculiar. The speakers, waiting for the audience to settle in, included a number of very big names from the intelligence community, including General Michael Hayden, by this time the former director of both the CIA and the NSA; James Woolsey, former CIA director; and Michael Mukasey, former Attorney General for George W. Bush.

And then there were the others. First among them was the facilitator and director of the Economic Warfare Institute herself. Dr. Rachel Ehrenfeld was a relative unknown who, throughout the long afternoon, would aggressively use her academic title at every opportunity, an unusual practice in this company. According to the available brochure, one of the other panelists would argue that jihadists were setting the wildfires ravaging Colorado that summer. Another, a former alternate director for the United States at the International Monetary Fund (IMF), would present a memorable anecdote involving complex terror scenarios not even Hollywood had ever produced.

In total, the panel included Doctor Ehrenfeld and eight white American men. At precisely 2:00 p.m., Ehrenfeld approached the podium. She opened her remarks with the announcement that the United States was target-rich for economic jihad, apparently a new concept for only a few of us in the audience. We, the uninitiated, exchanged nervous glances as she went on to explain the "cutting edge threats" that kept her up at night. She pointed out that both September 11, 2001, and September 15, 2008, were potentially devastating to the United States. One attack was the work of Al-Qaeda, a foreign enemy, and the other was self-inflicted by the management of our own financial institutions. However, Ehrenfeld said, we could not rule out the possibility that economic terrorists were: a) responsible for or b) learning from the economic collapse that precipitated the Great Recession. She also referenced the "flash crash" of May 6, 2010, when the Dow lost more than one thousand points in a few minutes, only to regain six hundred of them minutes later. Ehrenfeld reminded us:

> *Still, two years later, the joint report by the SEC [Securities and Exchange Commission] and the Commodity Futures Trading Committee did not rule out "terrorism" as a possible cause for the May 2010 "flash crash," and the entire financial industry still has no uniform explanation of why or how this event occurred. . . .*

EWI is of the strong opinion that threats to the US economy are the next great field of battle. Indeed, we are already at economic war with such state actors as China and Iran and such nonstate actors as Al-Qaeda and its affiliates. The future battlefield is vast: it not only includes the realms of cyber and space but also of banking and finance, market and currency manipulation, energy, and drug trafficking. The list could go on and on.[56]

Wait! We're at economic war with China? Most of us did not know that. Apparently the Chinese don't know it either because their government holds a large load of US debt. After the European Union, the United States is China's largest trading partner. And after Canada, China is the United States's largest trading partner.[57]

And what about an economic war with Al-Qaeda? Aren't we winning that one? We have Wall Street and the NSA. They have bitcoins and Waziristan.

The afternoon becomes increasingly fantastic. The EWI believes, Ehrenfeld informs us, that the US faces mass terror-induced electronic/economic calamity. The fact that this has not yet occurred, Dr. Ehrenfeld cautions us, does not mean it isn't going to.

When she finishes, she turns the microphone over to General Michael Hayden, now a principal at the Chertoff Group, a well-connected security consulting firm run by Bush's former secretary of Homeland Security, Michael Chertoff. General Hayden stands to speak about "the most dangerous weapons in the most dangerous hands—how much should we fear hacktivists achieving statelike capabilities?" The answer to this rhetorical question is "Quite a lot." Speaking as the former director of the NSA, he tells us that we want the government to go to the cyber-domain to defend us. In that domain, practically every advantage goes to the attacker because the environment is both insecure and indispensible. In other words, he says, he can't defend us without the proper weapons.[58]

Like Ehrenfeld, Hayden is frightening, but unfortunately, he does not tell us that afternoon what the proper weapons are. Nonetheless, as many in the room knew, the battle to acquire them is at that very moment heating up in the US Senate.

Between them, Ehrenfeld and Hayden establish a scenario in which the United States is unprotected from flash crashing at the hands of terrorist hacktivists waging economic jihad, and the next speaker is no relief. Daniel Heath, the former US alternate director at the International Monetary Fund (IMF) and currently a managing director at Maxwell Stamp, opens his remarks by inviting the audience to "Imagine this."

A foreign country holding about a trillion dollars in US debt demands an arrangement to swap it for the agricultural production of California. Alarmed, capital begins to flee the United States. It is Christmas, and a heavy snowstorm slams into the Northeast, knocking out the power grid. An act of sabotage hits the Washington, DC metro, and a couple of assassinations occur, both high-value targets and random ones. Finally, a biochem incident or two occurs, like anthrax or something in the water supply.

Heath just keeps on going. Shadowy parties might manipulate the price of oil and a real economic crisis would occur—like the one of

September 15, 2008. He suggests, then, that September 2008 was actually a jihadist plot. Probably.

What if terrorists aim to engineer a renewed financial meltdown? Is it possible? How would the financial system handle a massive attack on New York City? Is enough being done to buttress financial resilience— to limit the contagion of cascading failures throughout the economy? In what ways could different kinds of terrorist attacks succeed in destabilizing our financial sector and impair the real economy?[59]

All of these people are creative and emotional. Just imagine what they could do if they were talking about a real pending catastrophe like climate change.

David Aufhauser, former general counsel and chief legal officer of the Treasury Department, takes the floor. He announces the title of his talk, "Transnational Crime; Unholy Allies to Disorder, Terror, and Proliferation," and pauses to survey the room. Gauging the impact of that, he clears his throat and proceeds. Aufhauser speculates about an alliance between Iran, the Revolutionary Armed Forces of Colombia, and then-president of Venezuela Hugo Chavez. Among them, he suggests, they are about to create nuclear weapons for Venezuela. Terror, psycho-crime, drug-fueled guerrilla warfare, and jihad would come together for the politically purposeful annihilation of US-based banks. We must identify nodes in the corruption network and break the circuitry, Mr. Aufhauser urges everyone.[60]

After a few more presentations, Michael Mukasey wraps up as the final speaker. He is the hard closer, talking about legal perspectives on economic terror and the need for comprehensive electronic surveillance inside the United States. Essentially, he says, the law—whether national or international—is unequal to the task of controlling the contemporary technology of war.[61] The law needs to stay out of the way, he tells us. The rules won't work and the current regime is inadequate. Criminal law punishes after the act, but in warfare, we must often take action before the bad guys act. And the only way we can do that is to monitor them, so that we can intervene before they execute their plan for us. In addition, because we don't know exactly who the bad guys are, we're going to have to monitor everyone, and our "too big to fail" banks must help. The NSA, the CIA, Bank of America, and Citigroup will work together to protect all of us—and our data.

Why isn't this a comforting prospect? Perhaps because in 2012, when Dr. Ehrenfeld's conference took place, we were still recovering from the loss of our livelihoods that occurred as a consequence of the banks' last exercise in risk management during the run-up to the financial crisis of 2008. This reality, however, did not deter the Economic Warfare Institute from concluding:

> In dealing with new economic threats and circumstances, the law has a strong tendency to get in the way. This is not to disparage the law but, rather, to recognize that new circumstances beg some jettisoning of old principles and the creation of new ones.[62]

Yes, in a democracy, the law does get in the way. Of course, the logical next question is: get in the way of what, exactly? Even without an answer to the question, this statement from a roster of former US law enforcement and intelligence officials, many of whom took an oath to uphold the Constitution and the law of the United States, is unnerving.

This is the way a would-be dictator thinks. Angered by criticism of him that appears in a newspaper, the prospective autocrat wants to order the offending journalist arrested. But the law gets in the way. Frustrated by political opposition to a program he's promoting, the head of state imagines closing down the legislature. The law gets in the way. In the face of this aggravation, what is a clever tyrant to do?

Simple. Change the law.

The Cyber Intelligence Sharing and Protection Act (CISPA) is the new law that will supersede the obsolete statutes and principles now in place. In April 2012, three months before Michael Mukasey and his cronies spoke at the Economic Warfare Conference, the House of Representatives passed CISPA: legislation that would allow the keepers of the country's finances and infrastructure to share and protect the voluminous data they collect about their customers with America's military intelligence agencies and the Department of Homeland Security. And vice versa. The exchange could occur without warrants and beyond the reach of the Freedom of Information Act. That summer, Senator Kyl was doing his damndest to keep CISPA alive in the upper chamber, where it lacked sufficient support. The usual suspects opposed it: the ACLU, the Center for Constitutional Rights, the Electronic Privacy Information Center, the Government Accountability Project, the Electronic Frontier Foundation, and many others. For many months, those interested in the bill kept a campaign building, and Kyl's conference on that July afternoon was to alert the think-tankers to the urgent need for CISPA.

Ultimately, CISPA failed in the Senate that year, but in February 2013, Congressman Mike Rogers, Republican of Michigan, reintroduced it in the House of Representatives, just after the president signed his executive order on cyber-security.[63] As the timing of CISPA's reintroduction made clear, the executive order was regarded by the EWI and its friends as inadequate and flabby. In fact, they're right; it is a lengthy list of bureaucratic provisions that inspires neither committed support nor opposition—the kind of thing that gives government a bad name for creating metric tons of paper work for little gain. In brief, the order calls for a cyber-security framework, together with recommendations, reports, consultations, and inconceivably complex policy coordination. The drafters, however, did learn from the objections to CISPA: the executive order did not explicitly weaken existing privacy laws or require specific collection of data. Nor did it put an intelligence agency in the lead for the development of a cyber-security framework.

In the meantime, CISPA was making its way through the Congress, and on April 19, 2013, the bill once again passed the House with a few half-baked privacy protection amendments tacked on. It then headed for the Senate, where it had considerable support. Opponents called it "zombie legislation" because it refused to stay dead after it was defeated in 2012, even for six months.

There is a determination—a tenacity and relentlessness—about the campaign for CISPA that seems unusual, even now. The forces lined up behind it are impressive: General Dynamics, Lockheed Martin, General Electric, Northrop Grumman, SAIC, Google, Yahoo, the US Chamber of Commerce, IBM, Boeing, the Business Roundtable, Time Warner Cable, American Petroleum Institute, among many others. Bank of America and Citigroup support CISPA behind the veil of the American Bankers Association and the Financial Services Roundtable. Google, Yahoo, and Microsoft also signed on through a proxy: an industry association called TechNet. It's fairly safe to say that when you're on the other side of the issue from this league, you're at a distinct disadvantage.

For the American public, the stakes in the CISPA battle are high, which explains the resolve behind the corporate campaign for it. A tip sheet called "Tech Talker" explains what's in play here for the average citizen:

> *We're talking about the government legally reading your emails, Facebook messages, your Dropbox files, and pretty much anything else you had stored online, in the cloud.*[64]

That sums it up.

On February 14, the Business Roundtable (BRT) released a page of points explaining the position of its membership in support of CISPA:

- ► From our perspective, the missing piece of effective cyber-security is robust, two-way information sharing, with appropriate legal and privacy protection, between business and government.

- ► The current information sharing environment is not supported by strong legal protections to safeguard companies that share and receive cyber-security information from civil or criminal action.

- ► Furthermore, there are not nearly enough security clearances. In many cases, only one or two employees are cleared even within very large global enterprises, which create difficulties in communicating problems and acting quickly across global operations.[65]

The fight for CISPA continued through 2013.

In June, however, the CISPA campaign hits a snag: the Snowden disclosures. Edward Snowden begins releasing documents that expose the United States as the major cyber-attacker in the world. It's not the Russians, Chinese, or Iranians. Nor do Somali and Yemeni jihadists pose serious cyber-threats to American banking systems and electronic communications. The Snowden revelations are extremely inconvenient for the government-corporate surveillance complex because the hefty expenditures for the next round of cyber-battles depend on a persuasive and (at the very least) semi-hysterical cyber-terror narrative. Billions are at stake, and even if we already know the truth, the BTR and the NSA aren't going down without a struggle.

It is 8:00 a.m., on October 30, 2013. Washington is socked in for a dreary, drizzling day, as the cyber-security crowd gathers once again at the Ronald Reagan Trade Center, three blocks from the White House.

They will hear from a lineup of cyber-experts on the threats to critical infrastructure posed by "those who would do us harm." This clumsy reference to our putative antagonists will be used throughout the morning. As the experts talk about the calamitous consequences of a cyber-attack on Wall Street or our electric power grid, they never actually specify who is going to do this. Or why. In fact, the whole threat rests on the juvenile assumption that someone or some government—maybe Russia or a hacktivist group—will cause a disaster just because they can. Well, maybe they can.

Around noon, Keith Alexander sits down for an onstage interview. It's about fifteen minutes in, and he's behaving badly. He's trying to be flip and coy with his very pretty interviewer, Trish Regan of Bloomberg, but he's not coming off well. He's too old and geeky to be at all amusing in this way. Regan asks him a question about NSA capabilities, and Alexander answers, "I don't know. What do you think?"

She looks slightly perplexed. "But I asked you."

"And I asked you," says Alexander. He seems to be having a good time, but there's a certain amount of embarrassed coughing and seat shifting in the audience.

Silent moments pass, and Alexander begins to fluster; it seems that Regan is distracted by someone talking to her through her earpiece.

"General," she finally says, "this is just coming across the wire now, and we have no confirmation, but the *Washington Post* is breaking a story that the NSA has backdoor access to data from Google and Yahoo. Is that true?"

A hush falls on the anxious audience. Instantly, Alexander is a different person altogether. Gone is the flirty goofball who wants the pretty lady to like him. In his place is the cagey politician with an awkward yes/no question on his hands.

He looks earnest and deeply concerned as he replies. "This is not the NSA breaking into any databases. It would be illegal for us to do that. So I don't know what the report is, but I can tell you factually: we do not have access to Google servers, Yahoo servers, dot-dot-dot. We go through a court order."

Later, it turns out that the keywords in this answer are *server* and *database*. The *Post* report did not say that the NSA broke into databases and servers. Rather the newspaper reported that the agency taps into the cables that transmit data between servers. So with a barely perceptible sidestep, Keith Alexander gives a truthful answer to a question that wasn't asked and deftly misleads everyone listening to him.

It's impressive really. Alexander did this without batting an eye. Unless he knew that the story was about to break, he denied the truth extemporaneously without actually lying.

Regan retreats to safer questions: "Are we catching the bad guys?" she asks.

Alexander pauses again. This time, however, it is probably because it's not clear, even to him, who the bad guys are.

Except for one bad guy. Everyone knows who he is. Without saying so this morning, it is obvious that the only identified adversary for this group is Edward Snowden. His name comes up again and again. Around 10:30 a.m., one speaker becomes visibly agitated at the idea that Snowden's disclosures have undermined the case for closer collaboration between intelligence agencies and private corporations about cyber-threats—have quite possibly shot down CISPA for good and all. Larry Clinton, CEO at Internet Security Alliance, bursts out with his opinion that surveillance and cyber-sharing are completely distinct. Real-time, network-speed, machine-to-machine information exchange on cyber-threats has nothing to do with privacy, he asserts with exasperation. His head has turned red and he's looking at us as if we're stupid. "It's a completely different process," he winds up.

Then there comes a question from the floor: "So why do you need legal immunities?"

This is the question Bill Binney keeps asking. And the discussion at the Bloomberg event this morning shows that these people want legal immunities. The executive order is not good enough. The just-published cyber-security framework coming out of the White House isn't sufficient, either. There has to be legislation providing immunity. Threatened infrastructure—80 percent plus of which is privately owned and controlled—is not exchanging cyber-info without protection from the courts. This morning, after all is said and done, that much is very, very obvious.

The re-introduction of CISPA in the House of Representatives provoked an angry outcry from the civil liberties people. In America, when we focus, we tend to have a horror of intrusive government. This comes from the old days when the British quartered their horses in our parlors without asking permission, which would almost certainly have been refused. We pay taxes grudgingly; we suspect social programs of widespread fraud; we fear that a repressive police force will confiscate our shotguns someday soon. The only way to convince Americans to go along with the CISPA initiative is to crank up the terror machine again. This explains the quasi-psychotic tone of the briefing by the Economic Warfare Institute in July 2012, as well as the nebulous catalog of cyber-debacles alluded to at the Bloomberg conference.

Our history—the Red Scare of the 1920s, the internment of the Japanese during World War II, and the witch-hunts of McCarthy era—shows that however free and proud and fierce we consider ourselves, we willingly surrender our civil rights when we believe we're in danger. Each of these groups came under attack by a government that portrayed them as treacherous: the Reds of the 1920s were swarthy, low-class brutes, the Japanese were clannish Asians who were too smart for their own good and wore tiny little glasses, Communists were hirsute, ugly men in cheap brown suits and therefore untrustworthy for that reason alone.

After 9/11, all the old scare tactics came to life. Arab men, of course, became the objects of extreme suspicion. In the rapidly evolving national imagination, it was impossible to reason with them as representatives of other countries because they're fanatical and insane. They blow themselves up believing that they're going to paradise where they will debauch seventy-two virgins. In the meantime, they bugger young boys and one another. They have menacing headgear, and their women, whom they treat badly, wear sinister masks. To protect ourselves from these evil people, we allow surveillance, torture, kidnapping, imprisonment, and execution, which are—some of us admit—also evil.

John Kiriakou, the CIA agent who revealed America's official torture regime, reported his shock when he encountered the actual enemy in Pakistan in 2002: teenage boys who, when captured, cried and shivered and wanted to go home. He said he found himself asking: *This is it?* These are *kids* who can't even devise plausible cover stories for themselves. This is the mortal enemy America mobilized to hunt down and kill?

Now, admittedly, they aren't all kids, and they aren't all inept and untrained. The attacks of September 11, 2001, were highly coordinated, but then every propaganda campaign has a kernel of truth at its center. Effective official lies are always based on some credible fact. It's the extrapolation that reaches the realm of the fantastic. Let's think about it.

After the Cold War ended suddenly in 1989–1990, the United States was at a loss. The first President Bush was reluctant to declare the hostilities over for fear of economic disruption in the United States and Europe and lack of political direction afterward. Declassified memos of the last meeting between then-president Ronald Reagan, Mikhail Gorbachev, and president-elect George H. W. Bush in 1988 reveal that Reagan and Bush were stunned by the Soviet offer to disarm unilaterally. A report prepared by the National Security Archives, which obtained the memos, concluded that Bush was unwilling "to meet Gorbachev even halfway."[66] Nonetheless, of course, the Cold War ended without Bush's consent. America then struggled through the early 1990s with economic dislocation, later floating its prosperity on an ephemeral dot-com bubble and keeping such defense appropriations as were credible based on the feeble posturing of a dilapidated North Korea. Scanning the world for a believable enemy, the miserable Pyongyang was the best the Pentagon and the intelligence agencies could produce.

America had a brief skirmish with Saddam in early 1991, but then President Bush realized that this was playing with fire and got out quickly. The resounding defeat of the Iraqi military brought Bush only short-lived glory, and with a faltering economy, he failed to win re-election a year later.

And then came September 11, 2001. Tom Drake reported that one senior official at the NSA called the attack "a gift," suggesting that 9/11 revived the agency's argument for budget increases by showing the US public that real enemies continued to plot effectively against us. Although the attacks showed the utter uselessness of our alleged defense industries and intelligence services, both raked in huge budget bonuses afterward.

As the post-9/11 years passed, though, the terrorist threat wore thin. In March 2013, the tenth anniversary of the Iraq invasion came and went as barely a blip on the daily news cycle. Paul Wolfowitz appeared on CNN and made a pathetic effort to justify his role in the fiasco, but few remarked about his reappearance. George W. Bush, who presided over the eight years of terror warfare, never surfaced at all; it was as if he no longer existed. Nor did Dick Cheney return for interviews. In 2014, the official hostilities in Afghanistan will end, and it will all be over.

Socially and economically, the United States needs such a respite. Too much of the national wealth has been squandered on the unproductive expenses of war. In 2011, the last year for which we have comprehensive statistics, the US government spent more than $700 billion for defense and international security, more than the thirteen next-highest-defense-spending countries combined.[67] If that kind of out-lay is going to continue, with all the competing domestic deficits we have, we're going to need an imminent danger again very soon.

Beginning about eighteen months after the financial meltdown of September 2008, certain political forces began mobilizing about "the debt." Budget shortfalls in America would soon be crippling, they warned, and the House of Representatives began to obstruct all financial efforts to operate the government. The Republican caucus in the House refused to raise the debt ceiling without concessions from the White House. Those who rode into Washington with Tea Party support wanted cuts to Medicare and Social Security, programs the corporate elite have long referred to with the derogatory term *entitlements*. They threatened to shut down the government and refused to pass a real budget. The machinations became more and more creative. In August 2011, the Congress passed the Budget Control Act as a condition for raising the debt ceiling and avoiding national default. The act established the "sequester:" across-the-board budget cuts so draconian and disabling that even the House of Representatives, in the hands of the so-called fiscal conservatives, could never allow them. The Pentagon would take a virtually unprecedented fiscal hit.

But it happened. After four months of noise about the cataclysmic consequences of the sequester, the House refused to agree on a deficit reduction program, and the cuts went into effect on March 1, 2013. The Congress let them occur. In the fall of 2013, Tea Party renegades did shut down the government. If the defense industry was paying attention—which of course it was—fear and hate were flagging.

In Washington, though, a few prescient thinkers were getting ready and preparing a new menace: a truly frightening one. At GAP, where we represent whistleblowers from the NSA, the CIA, and the major US banks, we've learned that none of these institutions can be allowed to operate with the secrecy, privileged information, and latitude they already have. Using their current powers, intelligence agencies are already conducting wholesale surveillance of American citizens while wasting billions in taxpayers' money on boondoggle projects, which, if they worked, would be unconstitutional (see Trailblazer). For their part, private banks have been leveraging loans to a point where their solvency becomes an issue, while the individual compensation for senior managers bloats into breathtaking mountains of loot.

Despite this record of repression and recklessness, both the intelligence community and the finance sector are lobbying hard for CISPA. The last time this coalition of forces tried to pass the bill (in the fall of 2012), the legislation died. Its demise was lost in the uproar over the 2012 election that occupied everyone's attention after August. And then, in February 2013, the CISPA zombie came back from the dead.

After the Snowden disclosures stopped CISPA in the summer of 2013, we gained time to think about why it is that an official exchange of public and private data beyond the reach of citizens is such a bad idea. It's alarming because it forms the backbone of an alliance between two forces that already have great power, but which do not necessarily operate in the public interest. To be sure, at their best, they do: a democratic government acts according to the dictates of the majority while respecting the rights of the minority, and a private corporation strives to produce and sell the best possible services and goods in a competitive market.

Suppose, however, they're not at they're best. Suppose government is captured by finance, and finance is monopolistic and systemically fraudulent. Then suppose that a tenacious law enforcement official with a nasty secret in his personal life is investigating Corporation X. Should the secret come to light, the official could be neutralized, and the problems he or she poses for Corporation X would fade away.

Client No. 9, aka George Fox, called the Emperor's Club from time to time to request the service of prostitutes, for which he paid handsomely. On February 13, 2008, at around 9:30 p.m., a call girl named Ashley Dupré arrived at room 871 in the Mayflower Hotel in Washington, DC, to meet Client No. 9. Forty-five minutes later, George Fox arrived—by midnight, he was gone.

Dupré called the club then with an after-action report. This call from the Mayflower Hotel to the Emperor Club desk was recorded by the FBI.

George Fox was Eliot Spitzer, the former attorney general of New York. Over the course of his investigations into the fast and loose Wall Street trading in the early aughts, Spitzer had made serious enemies. One of them was Ken Langone, chairman of the compensation committee at the New York Stock Exchange. Another was Hank Greenberg, the former CEO of AIG, which in September 2008 was identified as the firm at the heart of the Wall Street collapse. Spitzer had pressured Greenberg to resign and Greenberg viscerally hated him.[68] Langone, too, openly detested Spitzer after the attorney general exposed him as one of the masterminds behind the spectacular

$139 million pay package given NYSE boss Richard Grasso for two years work at the not-for-profit, taxpayer-subsidized institution.

As Client No. 9, Spitzer attempted to hide his payments to the Emperor's Club. He often paid through a shell company and a small bank called North Fork, where he had also caused trouble. On one occasion, North Fork sent an unusually long and detailed Suspicious Activity Report (SAR) to the Financial Crimes Enforcement Network (FINCen), a branch of the US Treasury Department. Another bank, HSBC—also a Spitzer target—generated a SAR about the shell company, and somehow, the two came together.

We know that these SARs entered the databases of the NSA for data-mining purposes.[69] We also know that the FBI recorded Dupré's phone call about Spitzer in February 2008 and that was the end of Eliot Spitzer's political climb. The *New York Times* posted the headline "Spitzer is linked to prostitution ring" at 1:58 p.m. on March 10, 2008. In his book about the investigation, Peter Elkind reported that there was audible jubilation on the floor of the New York Stock Exchange and at Greenberg's Park Avenue office. According to Elkind, Greenberg received a stream of celebratory calls that afternoon, one of them from Langone, who knew details about the investigation of Spitzer that were not public.[70]

This is the kind of J.-Edgar-Hoover-esque nightmare that civil liberties groups cite when they envision the government/corporate cooperative surveillance to which we are subjected. Although Eliot Spitzer was not behaving admirably on that night in 2008, he was doing admirably good work for the public during the day. He was one of the very few public officials to challenge the reckless, value-free activities of the financial district in New York before 2008. Because of his personal misconduct, however, he is no longer working for New York state, and the damage to the public interest may go well beyond that. A fall from grace like his serves as a warning to public interest advocates who might otherwise take on the Greenbergs and Langones of this world. If your personal life is not presentable for one reason or another, you do not want to get yourself crossways with a corporate figure who may have access to the US government's database about citizens. In other words, if you're thinking about exposing waste, fraud, or abuse at a powerful corporation, think first about how the most embarrassing thing you've ever done will look on CNN.

Then there is Wikileaks, the antisecrecy organization that released the video "Collateral Murder" on April 5, 2010. The video, filmed on the morning of July 12, 2007, showed a street in Baghdad from above—from the viewpoint of the US Army Apache helicopter crew members as they shot the civilians scrambling for cover beneath them. One of the dead was a Reuters cameraman, and two of the wounded were children.

When questioned shortly after the incident, a military spokesman concealed the truth about how the Reuters cameraman died and said the army did not know how the children were injured. Through the Freedom of Information Act (FOIA), Reuters tried unsuccessfully to obtain the video for years, but the recording saw the light of day through only Wikileaks. In October 2010, financial reprisal against the site began. Moneybookers, an online payment firm in the United Kingdom that processed donations to Wikileaks, suspended the website's account.[71]

In December 2010, PayPal, Visa, Mastercard, Western Union, and Bank of America stopped processing donations to Wikileaks, and by January, 95 percent of Wikileaks's revenue had evaporated due to the banking blockade.[72]

Nonetheless, the website continued to publish the secrets of the US government. On November 13, 2013, Wikileaks posted the draft text of the intellectual property chapter of the Trans Pacific Partnership, a trade agreement being negotiated among the countries of the Pacific Rim. The chapter, negotiated in secret in the name of the American public, contained provisions favorable to the US private sector that could not pass the Congress.[73] If Wikileaks had not obtained and released the draft text, the public would not have known what the US government was negotiating in its name. Official harassment of Wikileaks continues.

Spitzer's history and Wikileaks's difficulties are cautionary tales about a capability and cooperation that can be used to target and punish political or corporate enemies, whoever they may be. There are also forms of government/corporate surveillance cooperation that target you. On December 11, 2013, the *Washington Post* revealed that the NSA piggybacks on Internet cookies to track users from website to website, compile their browsing history and target them for hacking.[74] An Internet company such as Google has almost certainly had occasion to attach its cookies to virtually everyone who uses the Internet with any regularity at all. In brief, the *Post*'s story showed the connection between the tracking done by commercial websites in order to target commercial messages to the consumers most likely to buy from them and NSA surveillance.

The story also revealed that the NSA uses cookies to track Internet users whose messages and activities are encrypted when they switch to unencrypted browsing.[75] In other words, Internet users trying to protect their privacy are singled out for surveillance by the NSA through Google. This collaboration is already occurring, and as the target population we lack the tools to stop it. Finally, consider the government/corporate electronic intrusions that may be coming soon. In theory and in practice, a database built on citizens' credit card history, banking information, email, Internet browsing record, and telephony metadata, held in common by intelligence agencies and private corporations, poses a genuine threat to privacy and dissent.

For example, Peter Van Buren, a whistleblower at the US State Department, asks that you think about what a telecom might do to you if you either got in its way or a surveillance partner such as the NSA requested a favor. Consider how you would live if nothing you ever did, said, or wrote appeared anywhere electronic ever. This is the scenario Van Buren imagines as potential reprisal to be visited upon you by Internet service providers if you should become a problem for them or their allies.[76] You are simply deleted and blocked from email, social media, and search engines. Without your knowledge or consent, online access to your public records is restricted. You are deleted from Facebook, Twitter, LinkedIn, gmail, and the rest. In the near future—if it is not the case already—you will have problems communicating with friends, finding a job, renting an apartment, buying a house, voting, getting a credit card, and as time passes, doing just about anything. You will be the last person on earth with a book of stamps and a box of stationery. With CISPA in place, you will have no legal remedy to digital exile. No matter what the damages, no one will be liable.

The danger of cyber-cooperation between the public and private sectors is deeper than a simple privacy concern. We're not talking about conspiracy theories here. We're not imagining the fantastic scenario of the government snooping on you just because. We're not talking about private companies using your personal Internet habits to target you for sales. Although these facts of life are not ideal, that's not really the point. We're talking about the collaboration between profit-making corporations and public agencies, such as the FBI and the NSA, which are empowered to target citizens for investigation and potential punishment. This threat is the real one. Secret collaboration between the power of force and the pursuit of profit is the point.

CHAPTER
5

Financial Reform: Dead on Arrival

Reason to be afraid #5:

Financial reforms enacted after the crisis are inoperable and ineffective because of inadequate investigations and intensive corporate lobbying.

Let's consider national security for a moment. This isn't as simple as it sounds because we're not sure what—exactly—anyone means by national security. Assuming we're talking about the planning and actions needed to ensure a stable future for the United States, the phrase should include the need to address threats to both our economic and our political systems.

If you're attending Senate briefings held by the Economic Warfare Institute, you will assume that the most serious threat to national security is the possibility of a hack attack on our banking system by unspecified enemies. In contrast, if you happened to miss the EWI events, and instead you're looking at the value of your 401k while wondering why your savings accrue 0 percent interest year after year, you'll know that the management and finance pros inside the banking system itself are the more likely danger. They are the people we ought to be scared of.

Speaking of terror, the weekend that began on Friday, September 12, 2008, was filled with heart-pounding panic at the Treasury Department, the Federal Reserve, and the Federal Reserve Bank of New York (FRBNY). Hank Paulson, secretary of the Treasury; Ben Bernanke, chairman of the Federal Reserve Bank; and Timothy Geithner, chairman of the FRBNY spent their time trying to devise a stop-gap financial plan that could avert the collapse of US financial institutions.[77]

Nonetheless, once the US government took the extraordinary measures necessary to forestall the cataclysm, pressure began building to provide legal immunities to financial institutions (among others) for whatever coordinated cyber-defense actions they might take with military intelligence and law enforcement. The institutions lining up for immunity, however, are the sites of the financial crimes that nearly finished us. The benign response to what the top echelon of bankers did stands in stark contrast to the reaction to the men who attacked us in 2001. Al-Qaeda leaders and anyone associated with them became the subjects of intense manhunts, detention, or execution. Americans who suggested that the War on Terror may have gone too far are still indicted and prosecuted. But those who threatened the national banking system and brought on the Great Recession avoided any direct accountability.

And now, in an impressive sleight of hand, terror—which was once our primary national security concern—has transmogrified into cyber-attack and then cyber-warfare, directed quite possibly at the banking system. This is the national security threat that Michael Hayden, James Woolsey, and Michael Mukasey tell us to fear now. And we should believe them; after all, they represented the NSA, the CIA, and the Justice Department. To combat this threat, we must extend legal immunities to the corporations that own American infrastructure. These companies want to be shielded from any lawsuit that could result from cooperation with US intelligence agencies about cyber threats. They include the same financial institutions that assumed so much risk they became insolvent and brought us to the eve of destruction only a few years ago.

Apparently, the prospect of lawsuits and/or criminal prosecution preoccupies the C-suites at the banks and the corporate owners of America. This seems odd, given that the Department of Justice uses its prosecutorial discretion systematically to spare them. In the wake of the financial crisis of 2008, not a single senior manager of a financial institution was charged criminally. At the same time, by 2014, the Obama Justice Department had indicted three whistleblowers from the intelligence agencies under the Espionage Act, subjecting them variously to investigation, imprisonment, and exile. Their alleged crimes? Informing the US public about CIA torture, NSA fraud, and unconstitutional NSA surveillance.

These two distinct reactions to crises—the suppression of dissent and the impunity accorded the managers of the country's largest banks and AIG—are the real threats to national life as we know it. Because the bizarre prosecutions and the silent tolerance of systemic fraud are incremental, though, we are not noticing that it's a dark new day. Today, there are no desperate people jumping from skyscrapers, no collapsing towers, no smoking ruins. There is very little panic, except for the poor souls at the Treasury Department over that terrible weekend in 2008. This threat is much more decorous and discreet.

It is Wednesday, April 7, 2010, and the Financial Crisis Inquiry Commission (FCIC) convenes in room 2123 of the Rayburn Building of congressional offices just across Independence Avenue from the US Capitol. The commission, appointed to identify the causes of the crisis of 2008, is expecting a high-profile day. At 9:00 a.m., the former chairman of the Federal Reserve Board will testify, and the place is packed. The press wants a good look at the expected exchange between the commission and Alan "the Maestro" Greenspan. The assembled reporters will not be disappointed. This morning Greenspan will make his 70-percent-right/ 30-percent-wrong remark that then headlines the websites of news outlets all day long:

> I mean, I think, I mean, my experience has been in the business
> I was in, I was right 70 percent of the time, but I was wrong
> 30 percent of the time. And there are an awful lot of mistakes in
> 21 years.[78]

When the FCIC chairman, Phillip Angelides, asks Greenspan if his refusal to regulate the financial derivatives market is part of the 30-percent-wrong quotient, Greenspan famously replies that he doesn't know.

This is passing strange because, without being nearly so clever as the Maestro, the rest of us know. Virtually everyone in America with a mortgage or a 401k is pretty sure that Greenspan's decision to leave derivatives unregulated back in the 1990s and early 2000s was the wrong call. As an indirect result of that decision, the housing market blew up, and the stock market crashed. Nevertheless, Greenspan rambles on in his self-exculpatory way for a good long while. By the time Citigroup whistleblower Richard Bowen testifies early that afternoon, the tone of confusion is already well-established.

Around 12:30 p.m., when the commission reassembles, Bowen and three others are seated at the witness table, and each gives an opening statement about the panel's topic: subprime mortgage origination and securitization. Bowen's statement is a bit different from those of his fellow witnesses, who imply that their employers' intentions were good but their risk assessment systems were flawed. Richard Bowen was the business chief underwriter for Citi in early 2006 with responsibility for vetting more than $90 billion of mortgage loans annually. During 2006 and 2007, he calculated that 60 to 80 percent of the mortgage-backed securities (MBSs) Citi was selling to investors were defective. When he testifies, he reveals that Citi was well aware of its time bomb of liabilities:

> *During 2006 and 2007, I witnessed business risk practices which made a mockery of Citi credit policy. I believe that these practices exposed Citi to substantial risk of loss. And I warned my business unit management, repeatedly, during 2006 and 2007 about the risk—risk issues I identified.*
>
> *I then felt like I had to warn Citi executive management. I had to warn the board of directors about these risks that I knew existed.*
>
> *On November the 3rd, 2007, I sent an email to Mr. Robert Rubin, Mr. Dave Bushnell, the chief financial officer and the chief auditor of Citigroup. I outlined the business practices that I had witnessed and had attempted to address. I specifically warned Mr. Rubin about the extreme risks and unrecognized financial losses that existed within my business unit.*
>
> *I also requested an investigation. And I asked that this investigation be conducted by officers of the company outside of my business unit.[79]*

At this moment, Richard Bowen is not telling the commission anything its members don't already know. In his written testimony, delivered a week before, he relayed the same message in detail. With that document, he provided evidence showing he warned senior management and the board about the poor quality of substantial percentages of the MBSs Citi sold to investors, among them Fannie Mae and Freddie Mac. These securities, Bowen asserted, did not meet the credit worthiness standards set by the bank. Because Citi guaranteed investors that they did, the bank could be obliged to buy them back if they went bad. If that occurred, Citi faced a staggering liability, for which it was unprepared.

Richard Bowen testified to the commission that he notified Robert Rubin, then chairman of the executive committee of the board of Citigroup, of the impending disintegration of Citi's MBS portfolio. Bowen sent his email on Saturday, November 3, 2007, because Charles Prince, then Citi's CEO, planned to resign the next day. The board was expected to name Rubin as chairman of the board. Bowen felt that he had to get the facts about Citi's hidden liabilities to the board that day because, as the end of the year approached, the chair and the chief financial officer would have to certify that the bank's internal controls were effective to meet regulatory requirements set out under Sarbanes-Oxley legislation (SOX), which passed in the wake of the 2001 implosion at Enron. Bowen was therefore warning Rubin that he could not sign such a certification because the internal controls at Citi were, in effect, broken.

Rubin did not respond to him. In fact, Richard Bowen says today that no one with responsibility for the SOX certification would speak to him before January; they did not want to know too much before they certified that the internal controls were effective at the end of the year. In January 2008, when senior management did begin to communicate with Bowen, it was to tell him not to return to the office and, subsequently, to terminate him.

Bowen's November 3, 2007, email, setting out the problem for Rubin, was attached to his written testimony and submitted to the commission.[80] Remarkably, the testimony received a polite audience from the FCIC, and then he was dismissed.

Even more remarkably, the FCIC seemed uninterested in Rubin's reaction to Bowen's email when he, Rubin, appeared the following day before the commission. In fact, he left the hearing room unscathed except for subsequent critical observations that he didn't seem sufficiently remorseful about what had happened in September 2008.[81]

Clearly, a prosecutor was called for when Rubin sat down to testify, but instead, the diplomatic commissioners went to considerable lengths to keep their collective eyes off the ball that day. Pointedly, Angelides did not ask, and Rubin did not volunteer, what happened to Richard Bowen himself after he sent Rubin the email. Thus, a senior manager's warning to the board chair of Citigroup that the bank had a $60 billion hole about to yawn open on its balance sheet eleven months before the US financial sector blew up disappeared with hardly a trace. After the FCIC interviewed Richard Bowen, the Justice Department never called him, and the SEC, in possession of his whistleblower disclosure since 2008, did not follow up, either.

Then, on September 21, 2013, exactly five years after the US financial world froze, William Cohan published a coda to the Bowen story in the *New York Times*.[82] The story asserted that the FCIC forced Richard Bowen to alter his written testimony, directing him to excise specific parts of it. Under threat that he would not be allowed to testify at all if he did not comply, Bowen removed the materials the FCIC identified from his written testimony. These included substantive references to his SEC disclosure, as well as his account of the Sarbanes-Oxley problems Citi faced in 2007. Representations to investors about the credit worthiness of the MBSs Citi sold, as well as all names and specific incidents and any reference to his own status at Citi, had to be deleted. The instructions to delete came from the FCIC deputy general counsel, who eight months later joined a law firm that counts Citigroup as a major client.[83]

Further, the transcript of Bowen's closed-door interview with FCIC investigators was placed under seal in the National Archives and cannot be released until 2016. By that time, the federal statute of limitations for fraud will have run out.

Undeniably, Bowen's warnings internal to Citigroup, his whistleblower disclosure to the SEC and written testimony for the FCIC were a problem for the US government as well as for Robert Rubin. Given the timing of the FCIC hearing, Bowen's statements were especially worrisome. At the end of March 2010, as he prepared to testify, the Treasury Department, a major post-bailout shareholder in Citigroup, announced the upcoming sale of 7.7 billion shares of the corporation's stock. The estimated value was more than $32 billion. As stated by William Cohan:

> The projected profit at the time, $7.2 billion*, would be among the largest from the government bailouts.[84]

The bank bailout of 2008 had been unpopular in many quarters, especially as millions of homeowners faced foreclosure and lost their homes. Politically, it was important that the liberal president from the Democratic Party show that the operation was not, in the end, a taxpayer subsidy to the same financial interests responsible for the recession. In other words, when Treasury sold its bank stock after these institutions stabilized, it was imperative that the sale price be respectable.

If Richard Bowen openly testified in April 2010 that Citigroup operations were contaminated by systemic fraud, there was a real possibility

---

*The government ultimately made about $12 billion.

that shares in Citi would not be attractive to investors shortly thereafter. In that event, Treasury would never have collected a $12 billion return on the sale of its bailout holdings. And if Treasury lost money, then the president and the government could be accused of using taxpayer funds to subsidize the already rich. On the other hand, if Treasury made money, then the bailout was a wash. A cost-free happy ending.

Making money. That's the key. In Washington, there are two vulgar sayings that guide the thinking of many who work here: 1) Follow the money and 2) It's the economy, stupid. Which brings us to Dodd-Frank and the financial reforms that never came.

To ensure that we do not have to witness the hearings of an FCIC II, the Congress and the Obama White House drafted the outlines of a reform that ultimately became the Dodd-Frank Wall Street Reform and Consumer Protection Act in 2010. The physical law called Dodd-Frank is officially 848 pages long. Matt Taibbi in *Rolling Stone* aptly describes the way in which the reforms have been neutralized by intense, never-ending lobbying from the financial world, first of the Congress and now of executive agencies responsible for writing the implementing regulations.[85] Taibbi compares Dodd-Frank to the fish reeled in by Hemingway's Old Man: "[N]o sooner caught than set upon by sharks that strip it to nothing long before it ever reaches the shore."[86]

By September 2013, five years after the crisis and three years after the law's passage, just about half of the regulations required to implement Dodd-Frank were finalized. To fully appreciate how significant this is, you have to take a glance at the law itself. Here's a sampling of section 165:

The Board of Governors shall, on its own or pursuant to recommendations by the Council under section 115, establish prudential standards for nonbank financial companies supervised by the Board of Governors and bank holding companies with total consolidated assets equal to or greater than $50,000,000,000.[87]

This section establishes an authority to prevent or mitigate threats to the financial stability of the United States through prudential standards (for managing risk) to be applied to systemically important financial institutions (SIFIs) with assets over $50 billion (such as AIG). As written, the law does not specify the content of "prudential standards," which would be established through regulation. Consequently, the work of the regulatory agencies is crucial, and the law is virtually useless in the absence of final-ized regulation.[88]

In December 2013, the regulators released the finalized Volcker Rule, one of the primary battlegrounds over the implementation of Dodd-Frank. This is the rule that will govern proprietary trading by bank hold-ing companies. The rule had to strike a balance between which trades would be allowed so that banks could hedge their holdings and which would be prohibited as speculative. Now the regulators say, the effective-ness of Dodd-Frank and the Volcker Rule depends on how the regulation is enforced.

> *Over the course of 71 pages, the respective agencies exhaustively laid out rigorous guardrails of what could and could not be permissible by large financial institutions like JP Morgan Chase and Goldman Sachs in the years ahead [under the Volcker Rule]. But agency officials were also direct in their concern about the upcoming challenge in ensuring that major banks would be held accountable in complying with the rule.*[89]

This means that first there's the law, then the regulation, then the agency guidelines for implementing the regulation. And then there's the ques-tion about whether banks will be held accountable for any of it.

It is significant that one of the regulations not finalized by the end of December 2013 is the one establishing capital rules for the biggest banks: the proposed leverage ratio. The ratio proposed by regulators is reportedly not popular with the big banks, who are lobbying against it by stalling it, pending agreement to a new framework by overseas regu-lators. This ratio is fundamental to preserving the stability of the finan-cial system in the face of systemic stresses such as those experienced in 2008. Five years after the crisis, however, there is still no agreement on a higher capital ratio.

At GAP we encountered Dodd-Frank directly through whistleblow-ers who came to us about the resolution plans required of certain types of institutions governed by Dodd-Frank. These documents, we found, were colloquially called "living wills." In the world of finance, the $50-billion-plus banks and AIG-like conglomerates are to develop them for imple-mentation should it become necessary to figuratively pull the plug. In part, this requirement was a reaction to the public perception that cer-tain large banks were too big to fail. And in part, the living will require-ment tells you something about the level of optimism shared by Senator

Dodd and Congressman Frank, the primary congressional authors of the reform, concerning the likelihood of avoiding another financial crisis. With the inevitability of death, the collapse is near, and the best we can do is get ready.

Our first problem is that the big banks and AIG operate the way Ford did when its directors realized that Ford Pintos were prone to explosions in rear-end collisions. Or the way the tobacco companies did when they realized that their product was carcinogenic. Because of half-hearted law enforcement on their beat, their risk assessment, to a large extent, consists of determining the cost of getting caught relative to the value of earnings accumulated before that happens. There's a major difference, though, between a Reynolds Tobacco shutdown and the collapse of JP Morgan Chase. The first closing costs jobs and dislocation in Winston-Salem, North Carolina, to be sure, but it would not affect the country as a whole. In contrast, if JP Morgan Chase goes down, the US economy is going down with it. Consequently, JP Morgan cannot be allowed to conduct business in the same shabby ways that the tobacco companies did.

Nonetheless, it does. A whistleblower, for example, reports to the SEC alleged criminal activity at the bank where she works. The SEC validates the whistleblower's disclosure but collects a fine instead of prosecuting the bank's managers or directors. The fines are substantial relative to the budget of the SEC, but they're not especially painful for the bank. The SEC benefits from fines, and the bank benefits from crime—probably some form of fraud. In the legal world this is known as civil compromise for nonviolent felonies. Both parties maintain a nonadversarial relationship as they work toward a resolution that benefits both. To put it crudely, on Wall Street, regulators would rather collect money than prosecute criminals.

The Clinton administration acknowledged this reality by establishing guidelines for deferred prosecution agreements (DPAs) for corporations, from which AIG and the SEC would handsomely benefit in the early 2000s. Under these agreements, a corporation simply pays the relevant government agency a fine and promises to do better. In exchange, the errant enterprise escapes prosecution.

To see how weak this approach is, think about the Internal Revenue Service (IRS) as the regulatory agency that oversees you and your taxes. Suppose you're an accountant with a salary, but you moonlight as an auditor for a couple of small businesses that pay you a total of $5,000 one year. You need the money, so you cheat on your taxes and don't report that income to the IRS, saving about $1,000. If you're caught—and you will be because the businesses you audited deduct your charges from their own taxes—you will owe the IRS the tax on the $5,000, plus penalties and interest—let's say $1,500—which you had better pay. Suppose instead that, when you cheat, you get a deferred tax-paying agreement: the IRS simply sends you a letter telling you not to do that again and fining you $50.

Are you going to cheat again next year? I might. That's how self-reporting and deferred prosecution agreements work for the big banks. The penalty—or fine—such as it is, is not a deterrent. And there are no prosecutions to speak of.

The American banking system is rotting at its core, and we have to be ready for failures of large interconnected financial institutions. Thus, the living wills required by Dodd-Frank.[90] At GAP, however, after seeing the way in which living wills are put together, we are guessing that most of them are rotten, too.

The first hole in the new regulatory regime is the Federal Reserve Bank (FRB). At the behest of the Obama White House, the Fed, an institution that presided over the collapse of 2008, gained greater authority as a systemic risk regulator in finance and is now one of the reviewers of the living wills. Not even the Congress thought this was a good idea—at first.[91] Christopher Dodd, quoting a knowledgeable observer on the issue, said:

> [G]iving the Fed more responsibility at this point is like a parent giving his son a bigger, faster car right after he crashed the family station wagon.[92]

Second, the law left bank holding companies much discretion in formulating these plans. Deloitte, for example, gave clients the following advice about drawing up living wills.

> Even as the regulations are finalized, keep in mind that regulators are prescriptive, not descriptive, in their guidance. They will not tell banks what to do, because each organization is unique. It will be up to the banks themselves to determine how to satisfy this requirement.[93]

Even before the regulations implementing living wills were finalized, the pros in the field knew this would be "regulation lite."

Third, the data in the living wills are largely self-reported, so the banks and the SIFIs have to be sure only that the numbers add up and the tables square. Little external oversight is involved, and if the plans are inadequate, the Fed isn't going to realize it until the plan has to be executed, at which point, it's too late to correct it. Submitting information that is insufficient to serve as an effective roadmap for bank dissolution, under the regulations, is not a crime.

To complicate matters, congressional oversight of the financial regulators is split among the committees on banking (Senate), financial services (House), and the agriculture committees of the Senate and House, just as it was before the 2008 crisis. As Treasury secretary, Timothy Geithner tried to remedy this, but he lost. He thought the banking and financial services committees should oversee all reporting on financial institutions and markets, but the agriculture committees wanted to keep their cut. They exercise oversight of the Commodities Futures Trading Commission (CFTC), which regulates financial derivatives. So long as the agriculture committees hold on to this function, its members are in line for campaign contributions from the finance industry, which can be quite generous. So the best Geithner could get was a joint task force.

This divided oversight is an illustration of how money talks:

> [F]inancial interests contributed $8.7 million to members of the House Agriculture Committee, compared to $7 million donated by agribusiness interests. For the Senate Committee the numbers were even more striking: $29.3 million given to members of both parties by financial interests, versus $10.8 million given by agribusiness.[94]

The SEC, for its part, reports to the banking and finance committees. These are among the largest committees in the Congress, and their members, too, are beneficiaries of the largesse of the finance industry. Members of the senate banking committee collected more than $36 million from political action committees and individual donors representing the financial and real estate industries during the 2014 election cycle.[95]

And there we have it. The financial reform that will not fix anything.

This is the puzzling thing: Michael Hayden and Keith Alexander, heading up the NSA, are certain that our banks must be protected from terrorism by collecting and storing personal information about all of us and freely exchanging it with US intelligence agencies. But a cold, clear look at banking (and insurance) shows that the mortal danger facing finance is the conduct of the industry itself. The NSA and the regulators, however, pretty much rely on what the industry sees fit to give them, which, by all accounts, isn't much. At the same time, if a corporation is caught misleading regulators or investors, a deferred prosecution agreement awaits, together with a fine that funds the lax regulator for not really regulating.

Nice.

Prosecution Deferred: Justice Denied

Reason to be afraid #6:

Systemic corruption and a fundamental conflict of interest are driving us toward the precipice of new economic crises.

In the early spring of 2010, my phone rang, and the caller ID read "Unknown." On the other end of the line was an AIG whistleblower. Until the 2008 financial crisis, AIG was a rogue elephant in the zoo of the US financial world, unknown to most Americans. After that, though, everyone who read a newspaper knew what AIG was. AIG Financial Products Division (AIG-FP), the London-based unit that took on the risk for the Wall Street banks, became a familiar villain in the developing story of fraud and corruption underlying the Great Recession of 2008–2009.

My caller spoke tentatively at first, without specifics, as cautious whistleblowers do, but she was concerned about the way in which the AIG compliance office at corporate headquarters worked. This was the office responsible for ensuring that the huge insurer did not break the law in any one of the 145 or so countries where it operated.

According to the caller that morning, the mainstay of AIG's compliance program was "a joke," and it had been for a long time. For years the program consisted mainly of a list of about four hundred email addresses for compliance and law enforcement officials around the world, many of which were defunct (either the addresses, the officials, or both). Whenever

AIG wanted to inform the offices abroad and their government counter-parts of a new legal or ethical obligation, AIG Compliance would blast out the news using this listserv. Then the office director would order the deletion of the plethora of bounce-backs and consider her mission accomplished.

Over the next few weeks, we started getting names and numbers of other sources at AIG who would validate the fact that much of the compliance work there was substandard, leading up to and away from the weekend in September 2008 when the financial captains at the helm of the banking world finally realized they had steered it off a cliff. The AIG allegations we heard were awful, and the people who made them were afraid to have their names used in any public way. All of the claims hung together, though. One corroborated another. And the charges were quite specific. Every source said that anyone who tried to notify the AIG corporate board about compliance problems before 2008 found him- or herself on the post–September 2008 redundancy list.

Everyone I talked to mentioned James Cole, who worked in the office as an independent consultant for the SEC. He was positioned in the compliance office, went to AIG board meetings, wrote reports, interviewed people, and generally hung around. The *Wall Street Journal* reported that this assignment earned his law firm, Bryan Cave, around $20 million, for about five years work.[96]

Sources at AIG pointed out that an independent consultant/monitor for the SEC in the compliance and regulatory office was a condition of a deferred prosecution agreement that AIG struck with the SEC, the Bush administration's Department of Justice, and the New York State Department of Insurance to settle allegations of aiding and abetting securities fraud dating back to 2000.[97] At the time, deferred prosecution agreements (DPAs) were typically used to deal with low-level narcotics cases, and the *New York Times* called the agreement "somewhat unusual in white collar cases."[98]

Under the terms of the DPA, AIG paid a fine and appointed Cole to report to the SEC and the Justice Department on compliance. In this position, he reviewed the dubious financial transactions from 2000 forward, structured by AIG that supposedly violated accounting regulations and securities laws. These transactions were developed and handled by AIG-FP PAGIC Equity Holding in London, headed by Joseph Cassano. At the time, Cassano was also the also the head of AIG Financial Products

Corporation, the unit that sank AIG, its banking counterparties, and the US economy in 2008.

Then US deputy attorney general Eric Holder established the first guidelines relevant to DPAs for corporations in 1999 in a document that came to be known as "the Holder memo."[99] In the years since then, the memo has been criticized for its failure to address the DPA scenario specifically and the nebulous standards it set out. Among other things, the Holder memo failed to define compliance or to specify the requirements for selecting external monitors of corporate governance. The lack of definition caused great power to default to prosecutors, and left the door open to more and more flexible DPAs. These agreements have increased in number substantially, surging to thirty-eight in 2007, up from four in 2003.[100]

Despite Cole's monitoring after 2004, AIG was once again in trouble with the SEC and the Justice Department by 2006.[101] The corporation faced charges of additional financial improprieties and bid-rigging but settled with a second DPA, despite the fact that one of the factors applied to assess eligibility for a DPA under the guidelines of the Holder memo is the lack of an earlier offense. Under the 2006 agreement, admittedly, the fine was much stiffer than that exacted in 2004: AIG paid $1.6 billion in 2006 and broadened the scope of Cole's monitoring authority. At that point he became responsible for examining AIG's controls on financial reporting as well as corporate governance in the compliance area.[102] In exchange for this deal and the two payments, the charges against AIG were resolved two years before AIG-FP was identified as the epicenter of the 2008 financial cataclysm.

As the AIG monitor, Cole was to file reports with the Justice Department and the SEC. The reports, which were pages and pages of nothingness, were secret, but we obtained those Cole filed with the SEC. They were not for public consumption even in 2010, when the American public *owned* AIG, or 90 percent of it. Also, in light of what had happened there, the fact that Cole's reports to the SEC in 2006, 2007, and 2008 were uniformly basic and abstract was important in itself. In August and September 2007, he issued 215 pages of stupefying, mundane recommendations that read as if they came directly from a fraud examiner's manual somewhere. There was no meaningful interpretation, no analysis of how the law applied to AIG, even in the United States, never mind how it might affect overseas operations. There was no review of the corporation's actual practices, nor of the adaptations required to ensure that the crimes addressed in the DPA did not recur. The whole job looked like a cut and paste, until page eight-seven of the September 30 report. There, Cole wrote:

> *The Derivatives Committee [of the AIG Board] should be responsible for providing an independent review of proposed derivative transactions or programs entered into by all AIG entities other than AIG Financial Products Corp. ("AIG-FP").*[103]

He elaborated this exemption further:

> *For derivative transactions or programs entered into by AIG-FP, the appropriate independent review of the proposed derivative transactions or programs should be conducted by AIG-FP.*[104]

If AIG-FP reviews AIG-FP's transactions, though, that isn't really an independent review, is it?

When Cole wrote this waiver in September 2007, we were just under a year away from the awful night when the credit markets froze in the United States because no one knew which, if any, of the commercial and investment banks were solvent. Technically, many of them were not; their huge trades in derivatives, based on MBSs then going bad, were insured by AIG-FP, and AIG, for its part, lacked the reserves to pay out on the worthless positions the unit had guaranteed. In the wake of the 2008 economic collapse, press attention turned briefly to Cole, but no information was forthcoming from him, and no one other than the principals ever saw Cole's reports to the Justice Department.[105]

It got worse. One night in May 2010, about 9:00 p.m., the AIG source called again in an audible state of shock. James Cole was about to be nominated by President Barack Obama as deputy attorney general (DAG) of the United States, she said. The DAG is the senior official at the Justice Department who is often responsible for the decision to prosecute in a particular case, based on initial investigations. At GAP the next day, we were incredulous. The information was correct. Obama announced Cole's nomination as the second in command at the Department of Justice.

The Senate refused James Cole a vote on confirmation all through 2010, the longest delay of a DAG confirmation in thirty years. Obama was determined to have Cole, however, and so, reportedly, was Attorney General Eric Holder, a long-time friend and fellow poker player. The president gave Cole a recess appointment on December 29, 2010. He was sworn in on January 3, 2011, was finally confirmed by the Senate the following year and continues to serve.

The lack of criminal prosecutions coming from the Justice Department in the aftermath of the financial crisis is remarkable. It is, in fact, a glaring lack of zeal on the part of Justice. Consider, for example, US attorneys' prosecutions in the past five years: Tom Drake and John Kiriakou found themselves under criminal indictment, but the bankers and derivatives traders seemed beyond the reach of law enforcement.

On the *60 Minutes* episode that featured Richard Bowen in December, 2012, Lanny Breuer, head of the Criminal Division at Justice then, tried to explain this apparent immunity. The response he gave was both condescending and transparently untrue.[106] Breuer insisted that the department prosecuted cases it seemed likely to win, and he pointed out that the standard of proof in a criminal case is high. Therefore, in many cases where wrongdoing was evident, it made more sense to reach a civil settlement than to try a criminal case and lose.

Justice couldn't make the case against Tom Drake, either though, and yet US attorneys prosecuted him. They were forced to drop three of four charges against Kiriakou, but they still brought them. The high-profile prosecution extravaganza directed at the wretched former presidential candidate John Edwards is also notable. Justice lost that one, too, but the department evidently decided to waste years of time and buckets of money on that. Clearly, there is something more than "winnability" involved in the prosecution selection process going on at Justice.

Attorney General Holder explained more candidly when he sat before the Senate Judiciary Committee under oath on March 11, 2013. There he admitted:

> *I am concerned that the size of some of these institutions becomes so large that it does become difficult for us to prosecute them when we are hit with indications that if we do prosecute—if we do bring a criminal charge—it will have a negative impact on the national economy, perhaps even the world economy. I think that is a function of the fact that some of these institutions have become too large.[107]*

For Holder this was well-plowed terrain. He had struggled with the issue of indicting corporations since writing his 1999 memo on prosecutorial guidelines for avoiding such legal conflicts. The memo was an early effort to find a way to reform corporate compliance and ethics practices without resorting to criminal charges and shutting down the company with its attendant impact on jobs and the economy.

One year after Cole, on behalf of the SEC, exempted AIG-FP from independent review of its derivatives trades, the US economy faced imminent collapse. On Monday morning, September 15, 2008, Lehman Brothers filed for bankruptcy protection: on that particular day, the firm held more than $600 billion in debt, much of it owed to other interconnected financial institutions.[108] The effect was dramatic. Less than forty-eight hours later, money markets were approaching paralysis, and banks, at that point highly leveraged and heavily dependent on overnight borrowing from these same purportedly risk-free funds, faced the prospect of illiquidity, unless the Federal Reserve stepped in to back them, which it did.

Shortly after Lehman failed, of course, AIG experienced its own crisis: the corporation saw a precipitous decline in the value of its credit default swaps. These were contracts that allowed investors to bet on the credit worthiness of debt based, to a large extent, on subprime mortgages. Among the largest bettors were major Wall Street banks, and AIG was massively exposed. Then, despite the various bailouts and the frantic machinations of Treasury and the Federal Reserve, the economy of the United States truly began to unravel.

At the time of the financial crisis, the operators of the nation's critical infrastructure—which we would have to say includes AIG—were not yet officially authorized to scan their employees' personal communications and their customers' data for the purpose of supplying it to the NSA. In the two years that followed all this, people phoned and emailed us at GAP with information about what had really happened inside AIG. Senator Charles Grassley also received crucial information about AIG from whistleblowers. It was very important that callers and emailers could be fairly certain their identities would be protected. They were communicating confidential information, yet that information was essential to the public interest. In some calls to us, whistleblowers were exploring the possibility of legal representation in the event that it became necessary. If they had been readily identified, they could have been subjected to ruinous retaliation, and as a rule, the more serious the disclosure, the more vicious the reprisal.

One of the initial calls from the first AIG whistleblower was from a personal cell phone to a land line, and the whistleblower gave me additional names and numbers to call for more information about the bogus AIG compliance program. This information was not strictly protected by nondisclosure agreements, but the allegations made were unfavorable to AIG, a firm that undoubtedly would be covered by CISPA as it is written. Callers described and documented incompetence, racial discrimination, lack of due diligence, parasitic and redundant contracts, cronyism, retaliation, and so forth. Management at AIG would have every incentive to hunt down the identity of that first caller. Over the ensuing months, I received at least fifty emails from her after hours—from her personal email account to my GAP account. Someone employed at an institution deemed critical to the nation's financial infrastructure was exposing improprieties in the firm's compliance office to an outside organization. Under CISPA, AIG would have found the whistleblowers, and not only that: they would have no legal remedy to address whatever reprisal AIG visited on them next. If telephone metadata for my cell phone were collected by the NSA and delivered to AIG, the corporation would have a comprehensive list of its best-informed critics.

The collaboration between government power and corporate wealth is already finely tuned, as the experience of the unfortunate Eliot Spitzer and the DPAs themselves show. If we allow it to become closer still, we will be losing whatever legal protections remain for the dissenters and whistleblowers who survive among us.

The bailout of 2008–2009 was successful in a sense. It averted an economic recession/depression much worse than the one that actually occurred. As the financial crisis deepened, however, the bailout itself created a profound conflict of interest for the US government that is unresolved even now. A number of analysts, economists, and accountants pointed this out in late 2008 and early 2009, but no one who mattered paid attention. The Treasury Department owned a majority stake in AIG, which the government would, at some point in the short or medium term, sell back to private investors. Would it make sense for Treasury, now the owner of this corporation, to reveal to the public—and thus to the market—that the compliance program at AIG was worthless?

No. It wouldn't. And Treasury was under enormous pressure. Populists in the United States, both on the left and right, opposed the bailout as a giveaway to financial institutions, so Treasury simply had to come out of the crisis without a substantial loss. Although this was manageable, of course, the processes behind it weren't credible. The Treasury Department was both the owner of the compromised banks and their evaluator. This conflict of interest leaves us unsure about the validity of the stress tests applied to the major financial institutions in February 2009 to determine their capacity to withstand a difficult economic environment. The administrator of the tests, the US Treasury, had a very specific interest in the outcome. The department would sabotage its own interests if it were to announce to the market that the shares it intended to sell of Citi, Bank of America, JP Morgan Chase, and others were junk.[109]

At the time the government bailed out US financial institutions in 2008, a number of politicians, activists, and interests expressed different objections. For taxpayers, it was galling that the same corporations whose greed and recklessness caused the crisis would be financially revived with public money. During the years previous, the bank managers, board members, and traders at fault compensated themselves with lavish salaries and bonuses, spoke with contempt about the average investor they defrauded, treated the capital markets like casinos, and generally lived large. Despite the popular resentment and anger at bankers and traders, though, between the administrations of Bush and Obama, the American government salvaged the wreck of Wall Street.

In doing so, they created a snare of conflicts of interest that has yet to be untangled. Many have been scrutinized and publicized since then. Some are simply an outrage in a country where competitive markets operate at all. The issues are numerous and complex, but the fundamental structural conflict of interest—the one illustrated by what happened to Richard Bowen, as well as by the positioning of James Cole—is unaddressed.

When the Treasury Department devised the Troubled Asset Relief Program (TARP), it acquired substantial ownership stakes in Citigroup, JP Morgan, Wells Fargo, Merrill Lynch, Morgan Stanley, Goldman Sachs, Bank of New York, and State Street Bank. Under a separate agreement, the US government acquired a 90 percent ownership stake in AIG. After the bailout, Treasury was to resell the shares it owned on the open market and recover for the taxpayer the hundreds of billions in cash and guarantees disbursed and committed in 2008 and 2009. To a large extent, the plan worked. The financial world stabilized and, at least partially, recovered.

According to Treasury, as of June 2013, 96.1 percent of the TARP funds had been repaid.[110]

This is a great success for the Treasury Department, the Federal Reserve, and for those who devised the TARP. The unfinished business, however, concerns law enforcement and systemic corruption. In order to resell the questionable assets acquired during the bailout, Treasury needed to ensure that the reputations of the corporations whose stock went on the market (and their officers) remained unsullied. The department could hardly sell its ownership shares of the banks or of AIG at par or better if the Justice Department were prosecuting directors, managers, or the corporation itself. Moreover, Treasury's sales would be most beneficial to the government (and the taxpayer) if all legal liabilities were settled without an admission of guilt. We can hardly be surprised, then, that no high-visibility prosecutions of megabank officers materialized. Nor should we be surprised that the civil settlements brokered by the SEC and the Justice Department typically concluded without either an admission or a denial of wrongdoing by corporate officers.

When the bigger picture clicks in, it all makes sense. Faced with systemic fraud in the financial and nonfinancial institutions that it owns, the Treasury Department will discourage the Justice Department from prosecuting. If cases of corruption and fraud had been marginal or isolated to a few divisions in a few corporations, they could have been addressed and corrected. Specific culpable managers could have been identified and prosecuted, but this was not an isolated occurrence. The fraud was systemic. It was not contained in a single institution, either. It affected the financial industry as a whole. Fraud was and is epidemic. No single bank could opt out of it. If, say, one bank went straight, it would show lower returns, capital would flee, the CEO would be terminated, and another one who could get it right would be appointed.

The government in 2009 owned a substantial part of this industry. How could prosecutions of the industry's officers benefit anyone? Because the fraud was institutional and integral, criminal prosecution would expose the fragility of the entire structure of finance. Jobs, mortgages, pensions, 401ks, and major fortunes could all have been devastated. Difficult as it might be to imagine, the damage might have been much, much worse.

We can debate whether Treasury should have done what it did in 2008 and 2009 all day long. It doesn't matter much now. As Allen Blinder shows in his book, *After the Music Stopped*, Geithner, Bernanke, and Paulson did not have other options.[111] They had to use the authority and machinery of the state to reclaim an economy on the verge of a break-down—more accurately, in the wake of a breakdown. What is imperative, however, is that they stop misleading us now about the economy and begin—at least—to break up the banks (and AIG) so that this does not happen again. Instead, the cover-up continues. It is ongoing still.

The New Regime

World domination is not easy. Sometimes, even your closest allies and strongest supporters are not really backing you up. For example, SAIC, Booz Allen, and the others want contracts for defense work (cyber and otherwise) to support the American empire. At the same time, senior managers at the Pentagon, the NSA, and the CIA want them to have these contracts because SAIC, Booz Allen, and so forth offer lucrative pre- and post-retirement employment opportunities. Suppose, however, that the most efficient and effective work on cyber-defense can be done relatively inexpensively in-house. Then there's a painful choice: a major contract for multiple billions and years to SAIC, with the vague promise of a huge cyber intelligence extravaganza of dubious legality ultimately in place. Or, a smaller-scale in-house operation that works better and costs much, much less?

The NSA has been going the first route rather than the second one for a while now. This is why intelligence has become staggeringly expensive. Like everything else produced by our economic system, SAIC concocts its surveillance programs in order to make money.

To help, everyone at the top of the NSA ensures that no one else comes along who can do what SAIC should do more cheaply or quickly or legally. The momentum of the system brings it down all by itself because, once the competition is eliminated, the profiteers paid to defend it will bilk it instead. The more successful they are at this, the higher their profits, but the weaker the system they depend on to generate their earnings. SAIC is doing what it's doing primarily in order to make money and not to protect the United States, although protecting the United States would safeguard its profits long term. As it turns out, the best defense money can buy isn't actually very good.

We all discovered this around 9:00 in the morning on September 11, 2001.

Here in the United States today, the state and the corporation go hand-in-hand, although the rituals of democracy remain as a reminder of how the US political system once worked. For at least one year prior to his ascension, the man who will nominally preside over us is obliged to speak to us with his sleeves rolled up, as an equal. Around the country, we gather in sweaty high school gyms to hear him beseech us for support. He tells us we're the best country ever—in the history of the world—and we sing our national anthem to the cacophonous tones of the varsity band. This is our political culture.

Occasionally, when we're in real trouble, the president or the Congress convenes a bipartisan commission of political appointees, closely associated with the corporate interests involved—whatever they are—and asks for hearings and a report. The commission is certain to be pretty tame, and its report will fall within the parameters of the politically acceptable.

For the rest, money talks. The shift from a democratic polity to a corporate security state is a long, slow transition that has gathered momentum in recent years, accelerated by the War on Terror, which justifies mass surveillance, and the financial crisis of 2008, which hastened the integration of finance and government.

In the long years since 9/11, there have been clear signals that we Americans are tiring of the War on Terror. As early as 2005, we were sick of the Iraq War: in June of that year, a poll conducted by CNN/USA Today/Gallup showed that nearly 60 percent of Americans opposed the war in Iraq.

In November 2008, we the public made clear our intentions about the War on Terror. We elected a president whose middle name was Hussein, whose initial popularity rested on his early opposition to the Iraq invasion, who promised to close the prison camp at Guantanamo, who spoke frequently about peace, and who deplored the extremes of economic inequality that had evolved in the United States.

Consistently, during the 2008 presidential election, Americans told pollsters that the number one priority for the country was the economy.[112] But the country did not tack back to economic reform after 2008. On the contrary, the reforms enacted through Dodd-Frank were bureaucratic and slowly implemented, if at all, and President Obama followed through on the bank takeover/bailout as designed by the Bush White House and Treasury Department.

Nor did the War on Terror fundamentally wind down when Obama arrived at the White House in January 2009. The hostilities became more clandestine, and most US troops came home from Iraq in 2011, but the national security state apparently increased its surveillance of citizens and its assassinations of suspected terrorists with drones. The surveillance state continued to contaminate the polity.

After Snowden began to disclose the reach of the national surveillance apparatus, those responsible—the president and congressional representatives—asserted their willingness to have a robust national debate about these practices. The president in particular expressed his opinion that the debate would be healthy in a democracy. For him and for other politicians who similarly weighed in on the issue, the enthusiasm for a debate was patently hypocritical. It was precisely these people who suppressed all public knowledge about ongoing domestic surveillance practices for years.

Let us make no mistake. This is not a debate. It is a battle for the centuries-long traditions and rights of democracy, a system of government that has served us well. The fact that a president, himself a constitutional scholar, would propose the abrogation of the Bill of Rights as a subject of polite discussion among presumably like-minded individuals is, frankly, outrageous.

Steadily, it has become legitimate for private corporations to conduct our wars and manage our defenses. To ensure their continuing control of lucrative public functions, they also purchase and manage elections, a practice that the Supreme Court condones. Obviously, it is late and getting later, but the struggle for an effective democracy is not yet over. Despite the rulings of the judicial system, the Corporate Security State still lacks a viable legal foundation to protect it from the rulings of the not-yet-compromised courts that operate in public. This is a deficit its proponents lament loudly, for despite the protestations of Keith Alexander, James Clapper, and James Cole, it is not legal for private companies to exchange bulk customer data with intelligence agencies without a warrant, and the wholesale warrants churned out by the FISA court are now a poor excuse for a dragnet data grab. Absent legal immunity for this collaboration, private businesses ultimately balk. After all, lawsuits are immensely inconvenient, and courtroom confrontations mean exposure. A plaintiff may demand documents and testimony, potentially revealing an unpresentable internal state of affairs. Among themselves, the directors of the Corporate Security State discuss their fear of lawsuits brought by small-scale nongovernmental organizations or by private citizens that will wreck both their reputations and their projected returns.

The campaign is on for a legal shift, to patch the chink in the armor of the Corporate Security State. Washington trade associations for banks and Internet security services are attempting to legislate the legal immunities of the state for their private clients and consolidate a regime that allows them to combine their data systems with those of government intelligence agencies. They are explicit about what they need, and the rhetoric associated with their claims is increasingly intense.

Have a listen to Mike McConnell, former director of national intelligence (DNI) and current vice chairman at Booz Allen Hamilton. He told his audience at a Washington, DC, gathering that two impediments obstruct the data consolidation of the corporate world and intelligence agencies. These are the lack of a legal framework for such collaboration and the lack of public commitment to cyber-warfare.[113]

"Are we facing a cyber–Pearl Harbor?" an anxious questioner asked from the audience.

"I hope not," Admiral McConnell answered, his voice lowered ominously.

Curiously, McConnell doesn't identify the enemy who will attack us. Nor does Keith Alexander or James Clapper or Michael Hayden. We are left wondering. Their alarms focus exclusively on the effects of the attack: our money will be worthless, our houses and offices will go dark, and we won't have any water or food. Plus, we'll run out of gas. Our briefcases will fill up with uncharged electronic devices. Blackberries, Androids, iPhones, iPads, Kindles, and laptops all will go dead. It will be horrible.

Who could or would do this to the United States?

Good question.

Joshua Axelrod, an expert on the parameters of US critical infrastructure, attributes the evil deed to "a James Bond super-villain type."[114] He says this seriously on National Public Radio. To be fair, Axelrod admits the American power grid is safe from full-scale attack because of its size and complexity. Only major state actors, like China, have the capacity to knock out the power grid of the United States and keep it out. He observes, however, that such governments have nothing to gain from such an attack. Like McConnell, though, Axelrod foresees some evil force preparing to do the deed anyway. According to him, we're lucky so far. The super-villain has not attacked: "Yet," he says.

It would seem as if the more likely threat is another banking collapse or the protracted loss of power somewhere in the coastal United States due to an intense storm caused by climate change. There is, however, little action on either front. Instead, the defense establishment is preoccupied by the potential devastation to be visited on our cyber-system by an imaginary über-thug.

Because Americans are inclined to be skeptical of such doomsday scenarios, the Mike McConnells of industry despair of achieving the controls they desire so long as democratic practices hold sway at all in this country. McConnell himself is reduced to predicting outlandish events like a "cyber–Pearl Harbor" at the hands—presumably—of Goldfinger or Pussy Galore.

Frequently, those who advance the integration of public and private cyber-capacity, like McConnell, bemoan the fact that it is difficult to scare Americans on a sustained basis about invisible digital attacks. The website crashing incidents that affect banks from time to time are not all that much of a mass inconvenience compared to, say, heavy traffic on a weekday morning, and people tend to forget them quickly.

In the field of American political hysteria and fear-mongering, the absence of an identifiable, individual demon is also a problem. In the hysteria over cyber-warfare, there is no Osama bin Laden, no Ahmadinejad, no Gadaffi or Saddam. Most of us can't even remember the name of the current Chinese premier,[115] so although we're vaguely afraid of China, we're not really sure which Chinese superman is about to attack us. Although historically it is true that we will relinquish our civil rights if we are scared, we have to know not just what we are afraid of, but also whom. The fanatical Arab men crashing gassed-up commercial airliners into skyscrapers have faded away, but we have no vision of our next enemy. And so, opportunities to save a government of the people remain.

The disclosures made by Edward Snowden create an opportunity to rethink the post-9/11 agenda of our national security agencies. The Snowden disclosures show not only the specifics of domestic surveillance but also the larger fact that in the so-called cyber-war, the US government is the primary aggressor. While claiming to defend the homeland, for example, the NSA is burgling and compromising the networks of other governments. It is clear from official reactions abroad that the United States is virtually unequaled in the sophistication of these offensives, not because other governments are naturally pacific and benign but rather because they lack the capability to do what the NSA can do.

Our government is creating costly and far-reaching conflict not protecting us from it, and the Pentagon has taken this aggressive stance while representing to us that the opposite is true. According to foreign policy and defense experts in Washington, DC, we are being (or are about to be) attacked by China, Russia, Iran, Al Qaeda, hackivists, and other unspecified parties who "mean to do us harm." The Snowden disclosures show that this claim is largely fictitious. No other government can do what the NSA does. Nor can Al Qaeda. Although it's true that a loosely organized group of fanatics can hijack airplanes with box cutters, it does not follow that the same people can construct cyber-viruses. The United States is leading the way, starting the race, and forcing the world to divert its scientific brainpower, technological expertise, and scarce resources into cyber-warfare. We are also creating enemies, from whom we must then protect ourselves.

This is not to make an unqualified swords-into-ploughshares argument. It can be a dangerous world. But because it is true that the United States is the most developed and technologically advanced nation in the world, that position should give us some leverage in determining the development path we and the rest of the world are going to take.

Keith Alexander tells us that our national security apparatus is compromised by Snowden. Let's take him at his word. Much of the agency's work must therefore be scrapped, and the NSA will have to rebuild its surveillance programs. Why not pause here, then, to evaluate them? Must we really reconstruct all this? Do we have to fund it? Do we want to start an international cyber-conflict or do we want to back away from it? We know what Generals Alexander and Hayden think, but this is nominally a democracy still. What do we as the public want to do? What are our priorities as the budget debate paralyzes the Congress and the national debt overwhelms our legislators' imagination?

We should learn from the consequences of the twentieth-century nuclear arms race. During World War II, the United States developed a nuclear weapon and used it. Twice. After the war, the technology spread to other countries. In the twenty-first century, there are eight other nuclear states: Russia, China, India, Pakistan, North Korea, the United Kingdom, France, and probably Israel. The international community is still trying to locate and secure these weapons, long after it was obvious that they should never be used. The genie does not go back in the bottle.

Now the NSA has developed malware and backdoors and viruses, which, until exposed, it was deploying abroad (as well as at home). Using the inconvenience of distributed-denial-of-service attacks on bank websites as justification, as well as wild speculation about a cyber–Pearl Harbor, the Defense Department seeks expansion of its budget and its authority for the collection of signals intelligence. The corporate-government complex also seeks to consolidate its prerogatives and shield its private sector flanks from public scrutiny behind legal immunities.

The struggle we are facing is not about privacy versus security, it is about democracy versus tyranny. Because we know now what we were never supposed to know, we have a chance to redirect the future of the United States.

There are things we must do, presented here in an order of increasing generality. First, CISPA must not become law—not in any form. Second, further mergers and acquisitions among megabanks must be prevented, and the trend toward an increasing size and reach of financial institutions must be reversed. Third, the NSA must be held accountable for its massive violations of the Constitution, and the illegalities must stop. And fourth, most generally, the continuing development and growing capabilities of information technology must be put at the service of the people and not the state.

In the spring of 2013, the zombie bill came back at us for the second round: the CISPA passed the House of Representatives again, with a couple of half-hearted privacy fixes tacked on. Yet the law as worded remains a threat to privacy and civil rights. It allows Google, Yahoo, and others to break their terms of agreement with you without penalty and without informing you.[116]

To ensure that the surveillance state, which already exists, cannot fuse its capability with that of the private sector, the specter of a massive lawsuit for illegal information exchange and surveillance must remain real. The degree to which the corporate-government complex is consolidating can still be stopped. Technology companies, which are, after all, still private and therefore fear an exodus of customers, are responding to popular pressure in the wake of the Snowden disclosures.[117]

The Big Six—Apple, Google, Facebook, Microsoft, AOL, and Yahoo—wrote to the chairs and the ranking members of the judiciary committees in both the House and the Senate to request their support for measures that would allow the companies to disclose the court orders compelling them to release customers' data to the NSA. The letter was a direct response to popular perception that these companies are complicit in state surveillance of average citizens. In brief, the Big Six—and the smaller hundreds—are still vulnerable to legal challenge from the public and they should remain that way. There should be no immunities. Period.

The same kind of loophole-free legislation should govern the banks, which continue to pillage the treasury as they try to recapitalize themselves. New legislation should prohibit bank mergers and acquisitions by the biggest banks in order to limit the domino effect that the collapse of one of these institutions will have. As Garrett Jones writes:

> No "unless in the judgment of FDIC the public interest would be served by such an acquisition," no "final rules implementing this legislation shall be passed no later than January 1, 2018," nothing like that. Just a ban, now.[118]

Next, the public and the press have to ask why the NSA is unaccountable. Its authorities lied on the record in open session to Congress. To the press, they repeatedly deny actions and operations later revealed to be in progress. Or they claim that oversight and safeguards prevent abuse of their databases, and then we find that these statements, too, are fiction.[119] Congressional leaders not only fail to investigate, they actively defend the fiction and contribute their own implausible whoppers—later exposed—for which there are no consequences. There was a time, long ago, when lying to Congress was a serious offense. You can say you don't know or that you cannot remember (see Alberto Gonzales, July 24, 2007) or that you don't want to incriminate yourself. But you cannot lie. Nonetheless, NSA authorities did.

After James Clapper lied to the Senate Intelligence Committee about the NSA's domestic data collection, Senator Diane Feinstein—who should be asking tough questions herself but is not—volunteered that he probably misunderstood the question. But the question was absolutely clear, and instead of backing and filling for Clapper, Feinstein should have requested an investigation.

Congress is handling the disclosures about the operations of the NSA very gingerly for two reasons. First, some of the information collected is legitimately classified and related to the national defense. Secondly, if the NSA is collecting data on hundreds of millions of Americans, then the NSA is collecting data on members of Congress, too.[120] If you've been in Congress as long as many of the senators on the intelligence committees have, you've probably got at least a couple of fund-raising incidents in your past that you would rather forget, and you do not want the NSA reminding you about them. Congressional leaders will only act on behalf of the people under great pressure from the people. The press did its part in highlighting Clapper's deception; popular civil society coalitions must demand accountability of the NSA and the Congress.

Most generally, we must establish where the data we are creating belongs and to whom. Both the CISPA promoters and Julian Assange are right about this. It is a new world now. There are few rules and those few are broken. The US government assumes for itself prerogatives it does not permit any other nation. Routinely and self-righteously, our government protests hacking incidents that are hazily attributed to China or Iran. Then we find that the NSA engages in commercial espionage, sabotages production in other countries, taps the personal communications of the heads of state of allied nations, and bugs the international delegations at the United Nations. When confronted, the responsible authorities claim that everyone else is doing it, too. Actually, they're not, though. They don't have the capability of the NSA.

Corporate elites seeking profits and legal immunities are promoting an unnecessary cyber-war. Once we move across this threshold, the culture of the military takes over, and the battle to retain civil rights is lost. The mentality of the armed forces is black and white. There are good guys and bad guys; friendlies and enemies. In this context, the good guys are most certainly Citigroup, Bank of America, AIG, and the NSA. The bad guys? The *Guardian* and the *Washington Post.* You and I. All nuance will be gone, and in a cyber-war everyone with a twitter account a combatant.

We cannot allow this shift. The first step toward preventing it is an awareness that it is happening. Edward Snowden's disclosures gave us that proof. As information technology advances, however, without international and national regulation, without ensuring that the province of profit remains private—deprived of the immunities of the public sector— the window for preserving civil rights is closing.

The United States was and is the great experiment in self-governance, and Americans are rightfully proud of it. But we have preserved it more or less for only a short time, given the long sweep of history, and even this is hard work. We tire of it. We say, "I'm not a terrorist, so I don't care if some faceless bureaucrat is reading my emails." But we have to care. Without our Bill of Rights, there is no freedom of expression. Without freedom of expression, there is no safe dissent. And without dissent, there is no democracy.

Acknowledgments

Much of what I've come to believe over the years in Washington is based on what I've been told and shown by whistleblowers. Some of them are named in these chapters, but many of them must remain confidential in order to protect their professional and personal lives. Retaliation against those who expose the truth about the American corporate security state can be ruinous.

In some quarters, whistleblowers are described as people who speak truth to power, but this cliché is inaccurate. Power already knows the truth and doesn't need to hear it again from anyone. Whistleblowers tell the rest of us the truth. We're the ones who didn't know it.

Edward Snowden is in a stateless exile *not* because he told the National Security Agency that it is spying on Americans but because he told *us*. Richard Bowen was ejected from Citigroup *not* because he told the board that the bank's internal controls were broken, but because he told the Financial Crisis Inquiry Commission—he told us.

We didn't know that our government is collecting our telephone data or that our banks may be periodically insolvent. We believed that electing a different party and president means a different course for the country that our taxes buy us security and a thousand other fictions.

Because of whistleblowers, we now know better.

As corporate power dismantled government regulation, we have come to depend on individual workers to tell us the truth about what is happening in the agencies that govern us and the corporations that own us. What they've told me is that justice in the United States is crippled. Much of what we thought protected us is already little more than theater, and the rest of it is going away.

For telling the truth about America, I want to thank Richard Bowen, Eric Ben-Artzi, Thomas Drake, William Binney, J. Kirk Wiebe, and John Kim.

For his example and wisdom, I must thank Louis Clark.

For his relentless negotiating skills, Tom Devine must be commended.

Jesselyn Radack's courage has been inspirational, and Kathleen McClellan's expertise, quick work, and quick wit were invaluable.

And Michael Neff, who is never without a great idea. . . .

And finally for Frank, who listened, much gratitude. Always.

Endnotes

1. Glenn Greenwald. "NSA collecting phone records of millions of Verizon customers daily," *The Guardian*, June 6, 2013. http://www.theguardian.com/world/2013/jun/06/nsa-phone-records-verizon-court-order. Accessed November 5, 2013.
2. Glenn Greenwald. "Low-Level NSA Analysts Have 'Powerful and Invasive' Search Tool," ABC News, July 28, 2013. http://abcnews.go.com/blogs/politics/2013/07/glenn-greenwald-low-level-nsa-analysts-have-powerful-and-invasive-search-tool/. Accessed November 5, 2013.
3. http://computer.howstuffworks.com/cookie5.htm. Accessed November 15, 2013.
4. Heidi Bogoshian. *Spying on Democracy*. San Francisco: City Lights Books, 2013, p. 203.
5. "Despite numerous pieces of evidence and intelligence-gathering opportunities, it [the NSA] missed the near-disastrous attempted attacks by the Underwear Bomber on a flight to Detroit in 2009 and by the Car Bomber in Times Square in 2010." James Bamford. "The NSA Is Building the Country's Biggest Spy Center (Watch What You Say)" *Wired*, March 15, 2012. http://www.wired.com/threatlevel/2012/03/ff_nsadatacenter/. Accessed November 5, 2013.
6. Jane Mayer, "The Secret Sharer. Is Tom Drake an Enemy of the State?" *The New Yorker*, May 23, 2011. http://www.newyorker.com/reporting/2011/05/23/110523fa_fact_mayer. Accessed November 5, 2013.
7. Barton Gellman and Greg Miller. "US spy network's successes, failures and objectives detailed in 'black budget' summary," *Washington Post*, August 29, 2013. http://www.washingtonpost.com/politics/intelligence-leaders-push-back-on-leakers-media/2013/06/09/fff80160-d122-11e2-a73e-826d299ff459_story.html. Accessed November 5, 2013.
8. Editorial. "Billions spent on spying come into focus," *Newsday*, September 8, 2013.
9. Shane Harris. "The Cowboy of the NSA. Inside Gen. Keith Alexander's all-out, barely legal drive to build the ultimate spy machine," *Foreign Policy*, September 9, 2013. http://www.foreignpolicy.com/articles/2013/09/08/the_cowboy_of_the_nsa_keith_alexander?page=full&wp_login_redirect=0. Accessed January 4, 2014.
10. Ultimately, Trailblazer was expected to cost about $3 billion.
11. Unpublished memo, General Michael Hayden to NSA staff, April 14, 2000.
12. Laura Poitras. "The Program," *New York Times*, August 22, 2012. http://www.nytimes.com/2012/08/23/opinion/the-national-security-agencys-domestic-spying-program.html?_r=3&ref=opinion&. Accessed November 24, 2013.
13. There are credible indications that the effort to spy on Americans actually began before September 11, 2001. After the release of court filings in the insider trading case against Qwest CEO Joseph Nacchio, the *Washington Post* reported that the requests for warrantless access to customer phone data came from the NSA to Qwest in February 2001, which was more than six months before 9/11. http://www.washingtonpost.com/wpdyn/content/article/2007/10/12/AR2007101202485.html. Accessed November 5, 2013.
14. http://www.nytimes.com/video/2012/08/22/opinion/100000001733041/theprogram.html, Accessed November 6, 2013.
15. James Risen and Eric Lichtblau. "Bush Lets US Spy on Callers Without Courts," Top of Form Bottom of Form *New York Times*, December 15, 2013. http://www.nytimes.

com/2005/12/16/politics/16program.html?pagewanted=all&_r=0, Accessed November 6, 2013.

16. Siobhan Gorman. "Spy data system a 'boondoggle': After 6 years and $1.2 billion, NSA still hasn't set up Trailblazer," *Baltimore Sun,* January 29, 2006.

17. Dana Priest and William Arkin. "A hidden world, growing beyond control," *Washington Post,* July 19, 2010. http://projects.washingtonpost.com/top-secret-america/articles/a-hidden-world-growing-beyond-control/print/. Accessed November 8, 2013.

18. Testimony of Alberto Gonzales, Senate Judiciary Hearing, July 24, 2007, minutes 4–7. http://www.youtube.com/watch?v=fTlgvWFKEPg. Accessed November 24, 2013.

19. Priest and Arkin.

20. Letter to President Obama on Security Classification Reform Steering Committee, April 23, 2013. http://www.brennancenter.org/analysis/letter-president-obama-security-classification-reform-steering-committee. Accessed November 8, 2013.

21. *Transforming the Security Classification System,* Report of the Public Interest Declassification Board to the President, November 27, 2012, p. 10.

22. Ibid.

23. Jaikumar Vijayan. "Cost of protecting U.S. classified data doubles over 10 years," *Computerworld,* July 3, 2012, 2014.

24. FOIA allows government agencies to withhold documents through nine exemptions and three exclusions: the material is classified and includes trade secrets, personnel information, or intra-agency deliberations, among others.

25. Barack Obama, Memorandum for the Heads of Executive Departments and Agencies. Transparency and Open Government, n.d. http://www.whitehouse.gov/the_press_office/TransparencyandOpenGovernment/.

26. http://www.sunjournal.com/node/815552. Accessed November 8, 2013.

27. *Transforming the Security Classification System.*

28. The Government Accountability Project was one of the organizations that signed the appeal.

29. Ibid.

30. Scott Shane. "New Leaked Document Outlines U.S. Spending on Intelligence Agencies," *New York Times,* August 29, 2013. http://www.nytimes.com/2013/08/30/us/politics/leaked-document-outlines-us-spending-on-intelligence.html?pagewanted=all. Accessed November 16, 2013.

31. "White House Statement: Visit by Brazil's Rouseff Postponed," September 17, 2013. http://blogs.wsj.com/washwire/2013/09/17/white-house-statement-visit-by-brazils-rousseff-postponed/. Accessed November 11, 2013.

32. "The department does ***not*** engage in economic espionage in any domain, including cyber" (symbols original). Barton Gellman and Ellen Nakashima. "U.S. spy agencies mounted 231 offensive cyber-operations in 2011, documents show," *Washington Post,* August 30, 2013. http://www.washingtonpost.com/world/national-security/us-spy-agencies-mounted-231-offensive-cyber-operations-in-2011-documents-show/2013/08/30/d090a6ae-119e-11e3-b4cb-fd7ce041d814_story_1.html. Accessed November 24, 2013.

33. Barton Gellman. "NSA broke privacy rules thousands of times per year, audit finds," *Washington Post,* August 15, 2013. http://articles.washingtonpost.com/2013-08-15/world/41431831_1_washington-post-national-security-agency-documents. Accessed November 11, 2013.

34. http://takingnote.blogs.nytimes.com/2013/06/11/making-alberto-gonzales-look-good/. Accessed November 11, 2013.

35. http://blogs.wsj.com/washwire/2013/06/07/transcript-what-obama-said-on-nsa-controversy/ Accessed November 11, 2013.

36. http://www.tomudall.senate.gov/?p=press_release&id=1319 Accessed November 11, 2013.

37. *Electronic Privacy Information Center vs. National Security Agency*, Appeal. Argued March 20, 2012. Decided May 11, 2012. US Court of Appeals. No. 11-5233.

38. Pub. L. No. 86–36, § 6(a), 73 Stat. 63, 64 (1959).

39. No. 11-5233 US Court of Appeals, *EPIC vs. NSA*.

40. Nicole Perlroth, Jeff Larson, and Scott Shane. "NSA Able to Foil Basic Safeguards of Privacy on Web," *New York Times*, September 5, 2013.http://www.nytimes.com/2013/09/06/us/nsa-foils-much-internet-encryption.html?_r=0. Accessed November 11, 2013.

41. The Constitution of the United States. Amendment IV.

42. Three-quarters of those surveyed said they thought that an air strike was likely to make things worse, not better. http://www.people-press.org/2013/09/09/opposition-to-syrian-airstrikes-surges/. Accessed January 5, 2014.

43. http://www.gallup.com/poll/1675/most-important-problem.aspx. Accessed January 5, 2014.

44. Ibid.

45. http://articles.washingtonpost.com/2012-10-23/world/35500278_1_drone-campaign-obama-administration-matrix. Accessed November 14, 2013.

46. Matt Spetalnick and Steve Holland. "Obama defends surveillance effort as 'trade-off' for security," Reuters, June 7, 2013. http://www.reuters.com/article/2013/06/08/us-usa-security-records-idUSBRE9560VA20130608. Accessed November 11, 2013.

47. Jean Jacques Rousseau, *The Social Contract, or Principles of Political Right*, 1762.

48. Daniel Patrick Moynihan. *Secrecy*. New Haven: Yale University Press, 1998, p. 93.

49. http://dailycaller.com/2013/06/13/jailed-qwest-ceo-claimed-that-nsa-retaliated-because-he-wouldnt-participate-in-spy-program/. Accessed January 5, 2014.

50. Scott Shane. "Former Phone Chief Says Spy Agency Sought Surveillance Help before 9/11," *New York Times*, October 14, 2007. http://www.nytimes.com/2007/10/14/business/14qwest.html?_r=0. Accessed November 11, 2013.

51. Ibid.

52. Ibid.

53. *Hedges et al v. Obama*, U.S. District Court for the Southern District of New York, No. 12-cv-331 and *Hedges et v. Obama*, 2nd U.S. Circuit Court of Appeals, No. 12-3176.

54. Authorization of the Use of Military Force Against Terrorists, a joint resolution of Congress passed just after the attacks of September 11, 2001.

55. http://www.nationofchange.org/blogs/lawrence-davidson/bad-precedent-and-bad-faith-1376936410. Accessed January 5, 2014.

56. Rachel Ehrenfeld, Kenneth M. Jensen, Editors, "Economic Warfare Subversions: Anticipating the Threats. A Capitol Hill Briefing," The Economic Warfare Institute, July 9, 2012. http://acdemocracy.org/wp-content/uploads/2013/02/Economic_Warfare_Subversions4_.pdf. Accessed November 11, 2013.

57. US Census Bureau "US Trade: Top Trading Partners—Total Trade, Exports, Imports." Washington, DC, 2012.

58. "Economic Warfare Subversions," p. 19.

59. Ibid., p. 29.

60. Ibid. p. 46.

61. Ibid., p. 52.

62. Ibid., p. 8.

63. Presidential Policy Directive 21. Critical Infrastructure Security and Resilience. February 12, 2013. http://www.whitehouse.gov/the-press-office/2013/02/12/presidential-policy-directive-critical-infrastructure-security-and-resil. Accessed January 5, 2014.

64. http://www.quickanddirtytips.com/tech/computers/what-is-cispa. Accessed November 11, 2013.

65. Testimony before the US House of Representatives Permanent Select Committee on Intelligence, in a hearing on advanced cyber threats facing our nation, Business Roundtable president John Engler, February 2013.

66. *Report: Declassified Documents from Reagan, Gorbachev and Bush's Meeting at Governor's Island.* National Security Archives, December 8, 2008. http://www.cfr.org/united-states/declassified-documents-reagan-gorbachev-bushs-meeting-governors-island/p17996. Accessed November 16, 2013.

67. http://www.washingtonpost.com/blogs/wonkblog/wp/2013/01/07/everything-chuck-hagel-needs-to-know-about-the-defense-budget-in-charts/. Accessed January 5, 2014.

68. Maurice R. Greenberg and Lawrence A. Cunningham. *The AIG Story.* New York: Wiley, 2013, passim.

69. Michael Isikoff. "The Whistleblower Who Exposed Warrantless Wiretaps," *Newsweek,* December 12, 2008. http://www.newsweek.com/whistleblower-who-exposed-warrantless-wiretaps-82805. Accessed December 10, 2013.

70. Peter Elkind. *Rough Justice.* http://money.cnn.com/2010/04/12/news/economy/eliot_spitzer_excerpt.fortune/. Accessed December 6, 2013.

71. David Leigh and Rob Evans. "WikiLeaks says funding has been blocked after government blacklisting," *The Guardian,* October 14, 2010. http://www.theguardian.com/media/2010/oct/14/wikileaks-says-funding-is-blocked?guni=Article:in%20body%20link. Accessed December 27, 2013.

72. http://wikileaks.org/Banking-Blockade.html. Accessed January 3, 2014.

73. "Leaked Treaty. Worse than SOPA and ACTA," http://www.washingtonsblog.com/2013/11/wikileaks-leak-tpp-treaty-world.html. Accessed January 3, 2014.

74. Ashkan Soltani, Andrea Peterson, and Barton Gellman. "NSA using Internet 'cookies' to find targets. Snowden-supplied files say Google software is especially useful," *Washington Post,* December 11, 2013.

75. Ibid.

76. Peter Van Buren. "*1984* Was an Instruction Manual." http://www.tomdispatch.com/blog/175779/. Accessed December 8, 2013.

77. James B. Stewart. "Eight Days. The Battle to Save The American Financial System," *New Yorker,* September 21, 2009.

78. Testimony of Alan Greenspan, former chairman of the Federal Reserve Bank, before the Financial Crisis Inquiry Commission, April 7, 2010.

79. Testimony of Richard M. Bowen III, presented to the Financial Crisis Inquiry Commission hearing on subprime lending and securitization, April 7, 2010.

80. Ibid. Exhibit 1, p. 19.

81. Eric Dash and Sewell Chan. "Panel Criticizes Oversight of Citi by 2 Executives," *New York Times,* April 8, 2010.

82. William Cohan. "Was This Whistleblower Muzzled?" *New York Times,* September 21, 2013.

83. "Cadwalader, Wickersham & Taft LLP, a leading counselor to global financial institutions and corporations, today announced the addition of Bradley J. Bondi to its impressive roster of top securities, litigation, and regulatory attorneys. Mr. Bondi joins the firm as partner in the Washington, DC, office." "Bradley J. Bondi, Former Deputy General Counsel of Financial Crisis Inquiry Commission and Counsel to Two SEC Commissioners, Joins Cadwalader Partnership," *PR Newswire,* December 1, 2010. http://www.prnewswire.com/news-releases/bradley-j-bondi-former-deputy-general-counsel-of-financial-crisis-inquiry-commission-and-counsel-to-two-sec-commissioners-joins-cadwalader-partnership-111124834.html. Accessed November 21, 2013.

84. Cohan, September 21, 2013.

85. Matt Taibbi. "How Wall Street Killed Financial Reform," *Rolling Stone,* May 10, 2012, http://www.rollingstone.com/politics/news/how-wall-street-killed-financial-reform-20120510. Accessed November 29, 2013.

86. Ibid.
87. http://www.usatoday.com/story/money/business/2013/06/03/dodd-frank-financial-reform-progress/2377603/. Accessed November 30, 2013.
88. The regulation that established prudential standards for SIFIs with assets over $50 billion was finalized in November 2011.
89. Donna Borak. "Toughest Challenge Is Still Ahead for the Volcker Rule," *American Banker*, December 10, 2013. http://www.americanbanker. com/ issues/178_236/toughest-chal-lenge-is-still-ahead-for-the-volcker-rule- 1064164-1.html?zkPrintable=1&nopagination=1. Accessed December 12, 2013.
90. http://www.federalreserve.gov/bankinforeg/resolution-plans.htm. Accessed November 29, 2013.
91. The White House "proposed giving this authority to the Federal Reserve Board, despite Frank's warnings that Congress would not support 'rewarding' the only agency that had the authority to head off the Great Crash by regulating subprime mortgages, but chose not to do so." Robert Kaiser. *Act of Congress: How America's Essential Institution Works, and How It Doesn't*. New York: Alfred A. Knopf, 2013.
92. Ibid., chapter 7.
93. "Financial Reform Insights. A blueprint for 'living will' requirements," Deloitte. 2010. http://www.deloitte.com/assets/Dcom-UnitedStates/Local%20Assets/Documents/FSI/us_fsi_bking_Living%20wills_081110.pdf. Accessed November 30, 2013.
94. *Act of Congress*, 91.
95. http://www.opensecrets.org/cmteprofiles/overview.php?cmteid=S06&cmte=SBAN&congno=113&chamber=S. Accessed November 30, 2013.
96. "In a statement made on the occasion of the introduction of legislation to reform the DPA process, Rep. John Conyers said, 'I have been troubled by the Justice Department's increased use of deferred and non-prosecution agreements because they have been shielded from public scrutiny and oversight. When the Department enters into one of these agreements and appoints an independent monitor, the public should be assured that the interests of justice are being served rather than the lining of pockets of well-connected cronies.'" [July 16, 2008.] Peter Lattman. "The US's Fly on the Wall at AIG. Monitor James Cole Has Been Privy to Inside Workings," *Wall St. Journal*, May 27, 2009. http://online.wsj.com/news/articles/SB123812186477454361. Accessed November 21, 2013.
97. Rachel Delaney. "Congressional Legislation: The Next Step for Corporate Deferred Prosecution Agreements," *Marquette Law Review*, vol. 93, pp. 875–904. http://scholarship.law.marquette.edu/cgi/viewcontent.cgi?article=4959&context=mulr. Accessed December 10, 2013.
98. Lynnley Browning and Joseph B. Treaster. "AIG and US Complete Big Settlement Agreement," *New York Times*, December 1, 2004. http://query.nytimes.com/gst/fullpage.html?res=9904E3D6113EF932A35751C1A9629C8B63. Accessed December 10, 2013.
99. "Federal Prosecution of Corporations" (Eric Holder, then deputy attorney general), Department of Justice, Washington, DC, 1999.
100. "DOJ Has Taken Steps to Track Its Use of Deferred Prosecution Agreements and Non-Prosecution Agreements but Should Evaluate Effectiveness," GAO-10-110, December 18, 2009.
101. *Securities and Exchange Commission vs. American International Group*, Southern District of New York, February 9, 2006.
102. Ibid.
103. Deferred prosecution agreements have been criticized for the discretionary way that monitors are chosen, which may or may not produce a competent expert in the business practices of the corporation.

104. September 2007 Monitoring Report of the Independent Consultant to American International Group, Inc. Unpublished, p. 87.
105. "The US's Fly on the Wall."
106. http://www.cbsnews.com/8301-18560_162-57336042/prosecuting-wall-street/. Accessed November 19, 2013.
107. Transcript: Attorney General Eric Holder on 'Too Big to Jail' Judiciary Committee. March 6, 2013, 3:15 p.m. ET. http://www.americanbanker.com/issues/178_45/transcript-attorney-general-eric-holder-on-too-big-to-jail-1057295-1.html. Accessed November 19, 2013.
108. Sam Mamudi. "Lehman Folds with Record $613 Billion Debt," *MarketWatch*, September 15, 2008. http://www.marketwatch.com/story/lehman-folds-with-record-613-billion-debt. Accessed November 25, 2013.
109. Matt Taibbi. "Secrets and Lies of the Bailout," *Rolling Stone*, January 4, 2013. http://www.rollingstone.com/politics/news/secret-and-lies-of-the-bailout-20130104?page=3. Accessed November 12, 2013.
110. http://www.treasury.gov/initiatives/financial-stability/reports/Pages/TARP-Tracker.aspx. Accessed November 13, 2013.
111. Alan S. Blinder. *After the Music Stopped: The Financial Crisis, the Response, and the Work Ahead.* New York: Penguin Press, 2013.
112. By Michael Cooper and Dalia Sussman. "Voters in Poll Want Priority to Be Economy, Their Top Issue," *New York Times*, August 20, 2008. http://www.nytimes.com/2008/08/21/us/politics/21poll.html?_r=0. Accessed November 12, 2013.
113. Keynote speech: Mike McConnell, vice chairman, Booz Allen Hamilton, Bloomberg Government's "Cybersecurity: Risk. Response. Reward." October 30, 2013.
114. http://www.marketplace.org/topics/sustainability/nations-electricity-grid-gets-test. Accessed November 13, 2013.
115. The current premier of the People's Republic of China is Li Keqiang.
116. Mark M. Jaycox. "CISPA Passes Out of the House Without Any Fixes to Core Concerns," May 1, 2013. https://www.eff.org/deeplinks/2013/04/cispa-passes-out-house-without-any-fixes-core-concerns. Accessed November 1, 2013.
117. Craig Timberg and Ellen Nakashima. "Amid NSA Spying Revelations, Tech Leaders Call for New Restraints on Agency," *Washington Post*, October 31, 2013. http://www.washingtonpost.com/world/national-security/amid-nsa-spying-revelations-tech-leaders-call-for-new-restraints-on-agency/2013/10/31/7f280aec-4258-11e3-a751-f032898f2dbc_story.html?hpid=z1. Accessed November 1, 2013.
118. Garrett Jones. "Expanding Megabanks: Is Impatience the Cause?" December 22, 2012. http://econlog.econlib.org/archives/2012/12/expanding_megab.html. Accessed November 2, 2013.
119. David Kravets. "6 Whopping Government Misstatements About NSA Spying," *Wired*, September 12, 2013. http://www.wired.com/threatlevel/2013/09/untruths-in-snowdens-wake/. Accessed November 1, 2013.
120. Tal Kopan. "Bernie Sanders to NSA: Spying on the Hill," *Politico*, January 3, 2014. http://www.politico.com/story/2014/01/bernie-sanders-national-security-agency-spying-101726.html. Accessed January 5, 2014.

Index

Priest, Dana, 17, 18, 19
Prince, Charles, 61
PRISM, 5, 20
"prudential standards," 63
Public Interest Declassification (PID)
    board, 18, 19
public trust, 19

Qwest Communications, 33–34, 92n13

Radack, Jesselyn, 7
Reagan, Ronald, 21, 51
Regan, Trish, 48
retaliation, 33, 34, 37
Reuters, 55
Risen, James, 11, 14, 15
Roark, Diane, 12, 17
Rogers, Mike, 46
Rolling Stone, 63
Ross, Brian, 31
Rousseff, Dilma, 21, 22
Rubin, Robert, 60, 61, 62
Russia, 29, 47, 48, 84, 85

Saddam Hussein, 51
SAIC, 12, 13, 14, 46, 79
Sarbanes-Oxley legislation (SOX), 61
Schumer, Charles, 17
search and seizure, 1, 6, 27–28, 31–32,
    37
search warrants, 1, 14, 27–28, 45, 81
Securities and Exchange Commission
    (SEC), 42, 61–62, 65, 67, 70–71,
    74, 77
Senate Agriculture Committee, 67
Senate Banking Committee, 67
Senate Intelligence Committee, 21, 86
Senate Judiciary Committee, 23, 35,
    73, 86
separation of powers, 21–22, 29, 32
sequester, 52
servers, 48
signals intelligence (SIGINT) team, 8
60 Minutes, 73

Snowden, Edward,
    disclosure results and, 83–84
    government response to, 30–31, 49,
        81, 84
    public disclosures by, 3–4, 9, 20–22
Social Security, 52
Somali jihadists, 47
sovereignty, 22
Soviet Union, 33
speech, freedom of, 6, 30, 32
Spitzer, Eliot, 53, 75
Sprint Nextel, 5, 33
Spying on Democracy (Boghosian), 7
Stamp, Maxwell, 43
State of War (Risen), 11
State Street Bank, 76
Stellar Wind, 13, 14
Suspicious Activity Report (SAR), 54
systemically important financial
    institutions (SIFIs), 63, 66

Taibbi, Matt, 63
Taliban, 35
Tea Party, 52
"Tech Talker," 47
TechNet, 46
telephony metadata, 4–5, 8
Terrorist Surveillance Program, 17
Thin Thread, 8–9, 12, 13, 14
Thomas, Charles, 31
Time Warner, 46
Times Square Car Bomber, 91n5
torture program, American, 31, 50
Trans Pacific Partnership, 55
Troubled Asset Relief Program
    (TARP), 76, 77

Udall, Mark, 35
Udall, Tom, 23, 24
Underwear Bomber, 91n5
United Kingdom, 85
United Nations, 5, 87
U.S. Chamber of Commerce, 46

About the Author

Delane Rouse/Rouse Photography Group, LLC

Beatrice Edwards is the executive director of the Government Accountability Project (GAP) in Washington, DC. She works with whistleblowers from government, corporations, and international financial institutions on issues of illegality, abuse, and corruption. For ten years, she was a contributing columnist to *The Texas Observer*, working under the pseudonym "Gabriela Bocagrande," and she received a Project Censored award in 2002. Currently, she writes for GAP's inhouse blog and for *The Huffington Post* about corruption and surveillance issues.

Ms. Edwards holds an M.A. from the University of Texas and a Ph.D. from American University; she speaks publicly about the need for whistleblower and witness protection, as well as strong anticorruption measures in public and private organizations. She has spoken at conferences in Bangkok, Delhi, Paris, Sao Paulo, Moscow, and Cali, as well as around the United States. In March 2013, she helped to establish an international network of whistleblower protection organizations.

About the Government Accountability Project

The mission of the Government Accountability Project (GAP) is to protect the public interest by advancing the rights of employees to speak out about serious problems they discover at work. To achieve this mission, GAP assists whistleblowers in making disclosures to institutional policymakers, the public, and the media. Over the decades GAP's staff has developed inhouse expertise in several broad program areas, including strengthening the legal rights of whistleblowers, increasing food and drug safety, ensuring safe and cost-effective cleanup at nuclear weapons facilities, enforcing environmental and worker protections, pursuing national security, promoting corporate accountability, and increasing accountability mechanisms in international institutions.

Since its founding in 1977, GAP has helped more than five thousand whistleblowers and expanded to a twenty-member staff in our Washington, D.C. office. We also conduct an accredited legal clinic for law students and operate a highly popular internship program.

Hundreds of whistleblowers contact GAP each year. Unfortunately, due to budget constraints, we are only able to take less than 5 percent of relevant cases that come to us, no matter how worthy they may be. Our goal is that whether we can provide representation, you will be better off as a whistleblower for having contacted us. If nothing else, we will provide a diagnosis of your options and attorney referrals. If you would like to learn more about GAP, please visit our website. To request GAP assistance in blowing the whistle or challenging whistleblower retaliation, please fill out our intake application under the Request GAP Assistance tab on our website.

Government Accountability Project
1612 K Street, N.W., Suite 1100   Tel: (202) 457-0034
Washington, D.C. 20006   Fax: (202) 457-9855
http://www.whistleblower.org
info@whistleblower.org

Berrett–Koehler
Publishers

Berrett-Koehler is an independent publisher dedicated to an ambitious mission: *Creating a World That Works for All*.

We believe that to truly create a better world, action is needed at all levels—individual, organizational, and societal. At the individual level, our publications help people align their lives with their values and with their aspirations for a better world. At the organizational level, our publications promote progressive leadership and management practices, socially responsible approaches to business, and humane and effective organizations. At the societal level, our publications advance social and economic justice, shared prosperity, sustainability, and new solutions to national and global issues.

A major theme of our publications is "Opening Up New Space." Berrett-Koehler titles challenge conventional thinking, introduce new ideas, and foster positive change. Their common quest is changing the underlying beliefs, mindsets, institutions, and structures that keep generating the same cycles of problems, no matter who our leaders are or what improvement programs we adopt.

We strive to practice what we preach—to operate our publishing company in line with the ideas in our books. At the core of our approach is stewardship, which we define as a deep sense of responsibility to administer the company for the benefit of all of our "stakeholder" groups: authors, customers, employees, investors, service providers, and the communities and environment around us.

We are grateful to the thousands of readers, authors, and other friends of the company who consider themselves to be part of the "BK Community." We hope that you, too, will join us in our mission.

A BK Currents Book

This book is part of our BK Currents series. BK Currents books advance social and economic justice by exploring the critical intersections between business and society. Offering a unique combination of thoughtful analysis and progressive alternatives, BK Currents books promote positive change at the national and global levels. To find out more, visit **www.bkconnection.com**.

Berrett–Koehler
Publishers

A community dedicated to creating
a world that works for all

Dear Reader,

Thank you for picking up this book and joining our worldwide community of Berrett-Koehler readers. We share ideas that bring positive change into people's lives, organizations, and society.

To welcome you, we'd like to offer you a free e-book. You can pick from among twelve of our bestselling books by entering the promotional code **BKP92E** here: http://www.bkconnection.com/welcome.

When you claim your free e-book, we'll also send you a copy of our e-newsletter, the *BK Communiqué*. Although you're free to unsubscribe, there are many benefits to sticking around. In every issue of our newsletter you'll find

- A free e-book
- Tips from famous authors
- Discounts on spotlight titles
- Hilarious insider publishing news
- A chance to win a prize for answering a riddle

Best of all, our readers tell us, "Your newsletter is the only one I actually read." So claim your gift today, and please stay in touch!

Sincerely,

Charlotte Ashlock
Steward of the BK Website

Questions? Comments? Contact me at bkcommunity@bkpub.com.

MIX
From responsible sources
FSC® C113845

Certified
Corporation
bcorporation.net